We can solve mysteries using reason, logic, and intuition.

SCHOLASTIC

LITERACY PLACE®

Copyright acknowledgments and credits appear on page 128, which constitutes an extension of this copyright page.

Copyright © 1996 by Scholastic Inc.   All rights reserved.   Printed in the U.S.A.
                                             ISBN 0-590-48945-3
              5 6 7 8 9 10   24   02 01 00 99 98 97

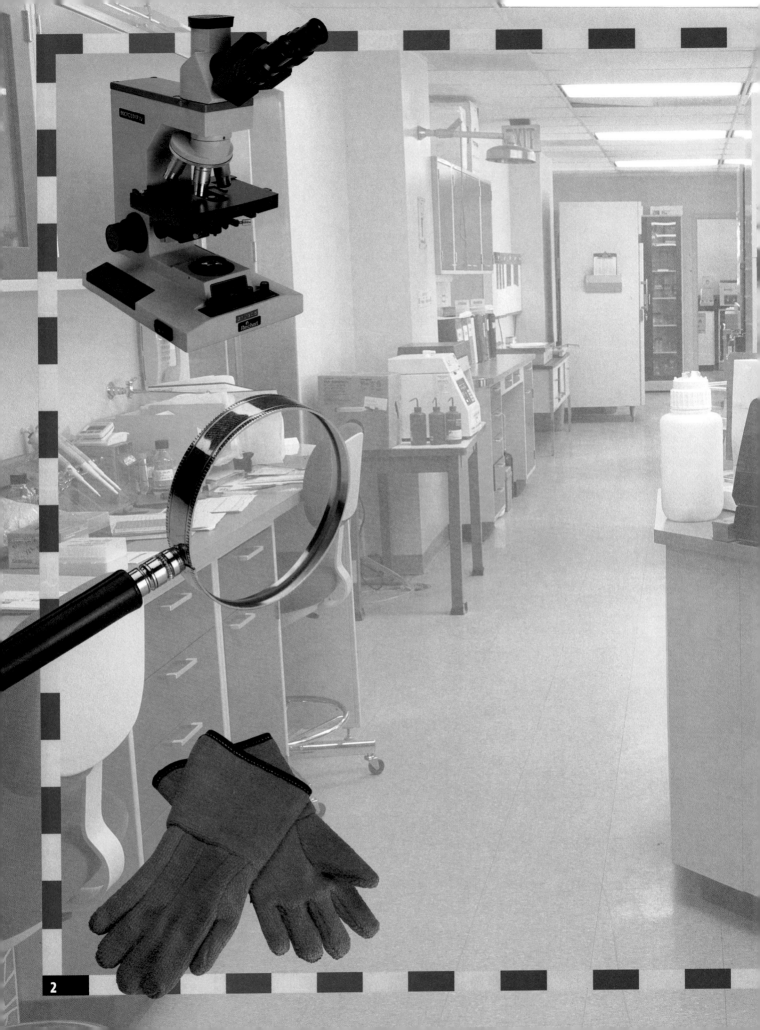

Investigate

a Detective Headquarters

We can solve mysteries using reason, logic, and intuition.

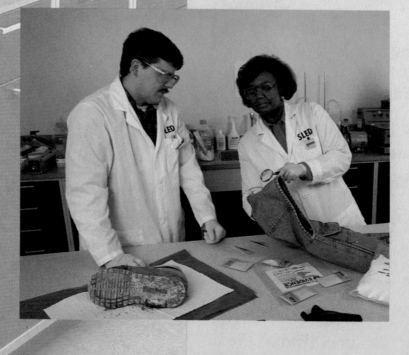

Guesswork

Making a hypothesis is part of solving a mystery.

SOURCE Picture Book

from
The Mysteries of Harris Burdick   10

by Chris
Van Allsburg

SOURCE Investigative Reports

Ask the Experts   20

SOURCE Poetry Collection

Some One   22

by Walter
de la Mare
illustrated by
Louise Brierley

from Peacock Pie

SOURCE Novel

from
Mystery of the Plumed Serpent   24

a dramatization of the book

by Barbara Brenner
illustrated by
Doris Rodriguez

W O R K S H O P 1

How to Create a Visual Mystery   40

Looking for Clues

Analyzing clues and evidence helps us solve mysteries.

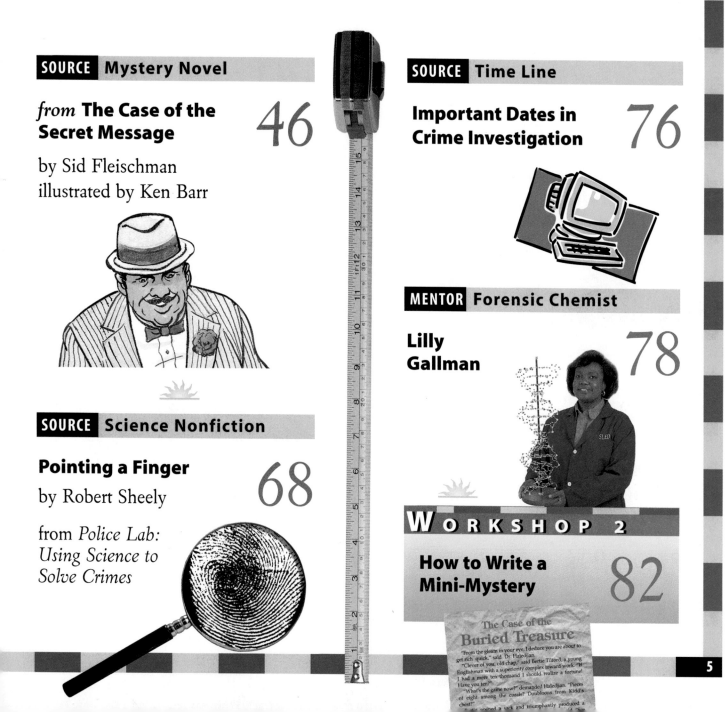

SOURCE Mystery Novel

from **The Case of the Secret Message**   46

by Sid Fleischman
illustrated by Ken Barr

SOURCE Science Nonfiction

Pointing a Finger   68
by Robert Sheely

from *Police Lab: Using Science to Solve Crimes*

SOURCE Time Line

Important Dates in Crime Investigation   76

MENTOR Forensic Chemist

Lilly Gallman   78

WORKSHOP 2

How to Write a Mini-Mystery   82

The Case of the
Buried Treasure

"From the gleam in your eye, I deduce you are about to get rich quick," said Dr. Haledjian.

"Clever of you, old chap," said Bertie Tilford, a young Englishman with a superiority complex toward work. "If I had a mere ten thousand I should realize a fortune! Have you ten?"

"What's the game now?" demanded Haledjian. "Pieces of eight among the corals? Doubloons from Kidd's chest?"

Real-World Mysteries

There are mysteries in the world that still puzzle us.

SOURCE Nonfiction

from **The Secrets of Vesuvius**

88

by Sara C. Bisel

SOURCE Reference Books

Unsolved Mysteries Around the World

112

PROJECT

How to Prepare an Investigative Report

114

SOURCE Newspaper

$200m Gardner Museum Art Theft

102

from *The Boston Globe*

Glossary 120

Authors & Illustrators 124

Books & Media 126

Trade Books

The following books accompany this *It's a Mystery* SourceBook.

Nonfiction

AWARD WINNING Book

Buried in Ice

by Owen Beattie and John Geiger

Newbery
Fiction

From the Mixed-up Files of Mrs. Basil E. Frankweiler

by E. L. Konigsburg

Mystery Novel

AWARD WINNING Author

Susannah and the Purple Mongoose Mystery

by Patricia Elmore illustrated by Bob Marstall

Adventure Novel

AWARD WINNING Author

Windcatcher

by Avi

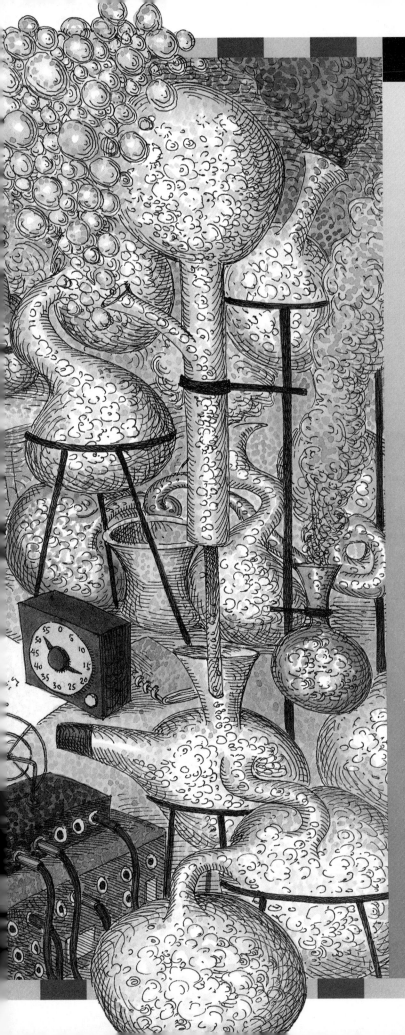

Making a hypothesis is part of solving a mystery.

Guesswork

Study some mysterious drawings. Find out what the experts have to say about one of them. Enjoy an eerie poem.

Meet clever twins who use guesswork to solve a pet shop mystery.

WORKSHOP 1

Devise a visual mystery and find out how observant your classmates are.

FROM

THE MYSTERIES OF

HARRIS BURDICK

BY

CHRIS VAN ALLSBURG

INTRODUCTION

I first saw the drawings in this book a year ago, in the home of a man named Peter Wenders. Though Mr. Wenders is retired now, he once worked for a children's book publisher, choosing the stories and pictures that would be turned into books.

Thirty years ago a man called at Peter Wenders's office, introducing himself as Harris Burdick. Mr. Burdick explained that he had written fourteen stories and had drawn many pictures for each one. He'd brought with him just one drawing from each story, to see if Wenders liked his work.

Peter Wenders was fascinated by the drawings. He told Burdick he would like to read the stories that went with them as soon as possible. The artist agreed to bring the stories the next morning. He left fourteen drawings with Wenders. But he did not return the next day. Or the day after that. Harris Burdick was never heard from again. Over the years, Wenders tried to find out who Burdick was and what had happened to him, but he discovered nothing. To this day Harris Burdick remains a complete mystery.

His disappearance is not the only mystery left behind. What were the stories that went with these drawings? There are some clues. Burdick had written a title and caption for each picture. When I told Peter Wenders how difficult it was to look at the drawings and their captions without imagining a story, he smiled and left the room. He returned with a dust-covered cardboard box. Inside were dozens of stories, all inspired by the Burdick drawings. They'd been written years ago by Wenders's children and their friends.

I spent the rest of my visit reading these stories. They were remarkable, some bizarre, some funny, some downright scary. In the hope that other children will be inspired by them, the Burdick drawings are reproduced here for the first time.

Chris Van Allsburg
Providence, Rhode Island

UNDER THE RUG

Two weeks passed and it happened again.

ANOTHER PLACE, ANOTHER TIME

If there was an answer, he'd find it there.

THE THIRD-FLOOR BEDROOM

It all began when someone left the window open.

THE HOUSE ON MAPLE STREET

It was a perfect lift-off.

Ask the Experts

The people pictured are well known in their fields for their special talents in investigation. They used their real-life skills to investigate the scene in *Under the Rug*, an illustration from *The Mysteries of Harris Burdick*. The experts explained the procedures they would follow to solve the mystery. Then they offered their best guesses—or hypotheses—about what is causing the bump under the rug.

Name

Barbara Steil
Private Investigator
Silverhawk
Investigations
Lincoln, Nebraska

James Campbell
Investigative Reporter
Dallas Times-Herald
Dallas, Texas

Myriam Rodriguez
Police Detective
Dade County
Police Department
Miami, Florida

Tim Leatherman
Exterminator
Dawn Exterminating
Edgewood, Kentucky

Lensey Namioka
Mystery Writer
Seattle, Washington

Job Description	Process for Investigating *Under the Rug*	Best Guess
As a trained private investigator, Steil has a whole slew of investigative talents up her sleeve. She uses different techniques depending on the case she's on.	Steil would begin by questioning the residents of the house. Then she would direct her attention to the rug itself, checking to see if there were any rips or tears in the fabric. As a last resort, she'd cut around the bump to reveal what was inside.	Most likely a small, injured animal unable to move.
When assigned to a story, Campbell has to make sure to check out every possible angle and source of information. It's his responsibility to get the facts straight.	Campbell would begin by carefully examining the police report, then questioning eyewitnesses and experts. He'd also look through the files in the newsroom to see if any similar cases had been reported in the past.	Some Texas towns have been known to be plagued by small burrowing rodents, like gophers. The bump is probably a gopher looking for food.
Police detectives have a special responsibility when investigating cases. Besides trying to solve the mystery, they've got to make sure the situation stays under control.	Driving to the scene, Rodriguez would be on the alert for suspicious activity. She'd interview any witnesses before proceeding to the location of the bump. She'd try to make the man with the chair stay calm.	Probably something harmless, like a cat.
When people are bothered by pesty critters, they call Tim Leatherman. He has to use what he knows about insects and small animals to make guesses about what could be causing the problem.	Leatherman would begin by questioning the man in the picture. Then he would rely on his powers of observation to study the bump carefully, listening for sounds and watching for movement.	Based on the size of the bump and his previous experience with cases like this, probably a baby raccoon lost from its home. Leatherman would use an oatmeal cookie to trap the animal safely and set it free.
While most investigators solve mysteries for the people they work for, Namioka creates them. And part of creating a mystery is using a logical thought process to come up with interesting solutions.	As a writer, Namioka studied the setting and character in the picture to come up with her theory. What kind of person is the man holding the chair? What kind of mood is present in the scene?	The man in the picture looked to Namioka like some kind of mad scientist. Her theory: the bump in the rug is one of his experiments gone out of control!

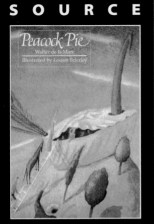
FROM PEACOCK PIE

By Walter de la Mare

Illustrated by Louise Brierley

Some one came knocking
    At my wee, small door;
Some one came knocking,
    I'm sure—sure—sure;
I listened, I opened,
    I looked to left and right,
But nought there was a-stirring
    In the still dark night;
Only the busy beetle
    Tap-tapping in the wall,
Only from the forest
    The screech-owl's call,
Only the cricket whistling
    While the dewdrops fall,
So I know not who came knocking,
    At all, at all, at all.

SOURCE

Mystery of the
Plumed Serpent
by Barbara Brenner
Illustrated by Blanche Sims

Novel

From

MYSTERY
OF THE
PLUMED SERPENT

A dramatization of the book by BARBARA BRENNER
Illustrated by DORIS RODRIGUEZ

CHARACTERS

MICHAEL	NARRATOR 2	MUSEUM DIRECTOR
ELENA	GRANDMA	MR. KANE
NARRATOR 1	BIG MAN	PARROT
	BLUE JEANS	

SCENE 1

NARRATOR 1: Michael and Elena Garcia live with their mother and grandmother in Number 24. The house next door is Number 22, which used to be a *bodega,* or grocery store. The store has been empty for years. But things change.

NARRATOR 2: Michael loves reading, especially books about Mexico, the country his father came from. While Michael and Elena's mother works downtown in an office, their Grandma sits by the window to see what's going on in the neighborhood.

NARRATOR 1: There are three other characters in our story—three strange men Michael and Elena have not yet met. But that will change . . . today.

ELENA: Trust me, Michael. Saturday is the day when things happen. In fact, I even smell adventure in the air.

MICHAEL: You smell the garbage truck down the street.

ELENA: You never want to have any fun. You just sit and read your old books!

MICHAEL: And you're always dreaming of things that will never happen!

GRANDMA: *Quiet, please!* Please make a little peace for me. Go out and play.

ELENA: Well, Michael? Do you want to help me find an adventure?

MICHAEL: Okay, I'll come. But you know nothing interesting ever happens in this neighborhood.

NARRATOR 2: But something interesting is happening. Someone is moving into the empty building next door.

NARRATOR 1: Michael and Elena run outside and look in the back of the moving van. It is filled with large boxes and a strange smell. They try to get a close look, but are stopped by a threatening voice.

BIG MAN: Stand aside!

NARRATOR 2: The voice belongs to a creepy, big man in dark sunglasses.

BIG MAN: Get out of the way!

NARRATOR 1: Michael and Elena stand back and watch moving men unload crates from the truck. The crates have Spanish writing on the sides.

NARRATOR 2: Michael and Elena hear a voice from inside one of the boxes and hurry over to inspect it.

ELENA: It's a parrot!

MICHAEL: I bet this is going to be a pet store!

NARRATOR 1: Michael and Elena enter the store to search for more animals. They don't see any movers, but they hear crates being dragged around upstairs.

NARRATOR 2: Just then, a very tall man in blue jeans, with bushy hair and a beard comes down the stairs. He doesn't look at all friendly.

BLUE JEANS: We're not open yet. Come back another time.

NARRATOR 1: While they talk, the big man comes down the stairs.

BIG MAN: Let them stay. We don't want people to think we aren't interested in customers.

NARRATOR 1: Michael and Elena don't care that the men aren't friendly. They feel like they are behind the scenes at a zoo.

ELENA: Excuse me, sir. Could you tell me what kind of lizard this is?

BLUE JEANS: A chameleon.

MICHAEL: But—

BLUE JEANS: Something wrong, kid?

MICHAEL: Uh, no. Nothing.

NARRATOR 2: The big parrot in the box keeps repeating the same thing over and over again.

PARROT: Catch a cold, catch a cold!

MICHAEL: What *kind* of snakes are these?

NARRATOR 2: Big Man glances at the snakes.

BIG MAN: Regular snakes. Very dangerous. They'll squeeze the life right out of you.

BLUE JEANS: We're locking up now. You can come back again.

SCENE 2

MICHAEL: That's funny. They're not selling cages, or leashes, or pet food. And there's something else. Those two guys aren't pet-shop people.

ELENA: How do you know that, great detective?

MICHAEL: Because they don't know anything about animals. The lizard you were looking at? That guy said it was a chameleon. But it's an iguana.

ELENA: So? He made one mistake.

MICHAEL: No, they made three. Those snakes I asked the big man about are boa constrictors. They're not really dangerous to humans. Besides, any pet-shop owner should know the names of his animals. There are over 200 kinds of snakes in the world, but there's no such thing as a "regular snake!"

SCENE 3

NARRATOR 1: When Michael and Elena come home from school on Monday, Grandma is reading the Spanish-language newspaper, as she does every day. Today, she is reading something a little out of the ordinary.

GRANDMA: Ha! Now that's a story!

ELENA: What is it, Grandma?

NARRATOR 2: Grandma translates from the Spanish for them.

GRANDMA: "The Mexican government is worried about smuggling taking place across the border. . . . Smugglers dig up old treasure from ancient Mexico. It is sold to art dealers for a lot of money. . . . People from the museum say it must be part of the treasure of Montezuma. . . . The Spanish explorer Cortes left it behind when he left Mexico in 1520. . . . The police from the United States and Mexico are helping each other track down these thieves and bring the treasure back to Mexico."

MICHAEL: Imagine if we lived in Mexico. We'd have a real chance of finding treasure if we dug around.

ELENA: Mexico, Mexico, Mexico. You think everything is better there.

GRANDMA: Here is something else. It says that they think the treasure is coming by airplane here to New York City. And the Mexican government has offered a reward of $5,000 to anyone who has information.

NARRATOR 1: Michael thinks it would be great to get the $5,000 reward. It would help his mother so much. But he doesn't say anything.

ELENA: Michael, I want to go back to that pet shop to look around.

MICHAEL: Go ahead. I'll be down in a few minutes, after I do some reading.

NARRATOR 2: The first thing Elena notices next door is a small sign in the window that says, "Pet Shop."

ELENA: "Pet Shop?" What a name! If I wanted people to come to my store, I'd call it "Jungleland" or "Wild World."

NARRATOR 1: Elena enters the store, and is relieved to find that neither Big Man nor Blue Jeans is around.

PARROT: Catch a cold, catch a cold!

NARRATOR 2: Elena plays with the caged monkey, feeding it some fruit she brought from home.

ELENA: Here you go, nice boy. . . . What? Finished already?

NARRATOR 1: The monkey does something very strange. He goes to the corner of his cage, scrapes away the paper and wood shavings on the bottom, and grabs something from under the paper. Then he runs back to Elena.

ELENA: Oh! I get it. You're giving me a present! Thank you!

NARRATOR 2: Elena looks down into her palm at a small gold animal with glass eyes. It's a small sculpture of a snake—with feathers. Elena thinks someone must have lost it while playing with the monkey.

NARRATOR 1: Elena knows she should give the snake to the pet-shop owners. Maybe they would know who it belongs to. She hears the men walking around on the second floor, so she starts to climb the stairs. Suddenly, Blue Jeans appears and grabs her by the arm.

BLUE JEANS: Where do you think you're going? No one's allowed up here!

NARRATOR 2: Blue Jeans seems so mean that Elena changes her mind about giving him the snake.

ELENA: Never mind. It's nothing.

SCENE 4

NARRATOR 1: Elena runs out of the store straight into Michael, who is on his way down to meet her.

ELENA: Michael! They—I was going up, and Blue Jeans grabbed my arm.

MICHAEL: They have no right to touch you! I'm going in there to tell them off!

NARRATOR 2: But when they get back to the store, it is closed—and locked up. So Michael and Elena go home.

MICHAEL: Listen, I found out something while I was reading. Did you know that every type of animal in that store lives in Mexico?

ELENA: So what?

MICHAEL: It means something. I just don't know what it is yet.

ELENA: You have Mexico on the brain. While you were reading, I found this! The monkey in the pet shop gave it to me.

NARRATOR 1: Elena hands Michael the snake sculpture, and he is very quiet. He turns it over and over, staring at it.

ELENA: What's the matter?

MICHAEL: This may be the answer. Two guys have a pet shop, but they don't know anything about animals. And they don't really seem to want any business. Why? Because their store is a front for another business. Bringing something in from Mexico. Something they can hide in the shipments of animals.

ELENA: Something illegal?

MICHAEL: Maybe even Montezuma's treasure!

ELENA: So you think Big Man and Blue Jeans are smugglers?

MICHAEL: Maybe. This snake isn't a piece of junk jewelry. I'll bet it's real gold. Your monkey may have given us a clue to the Mexican treasure!

ELENA: How do you think the monkey got it, anyway?

MICHAEL: Monkeys are naturally curious. But those guys probably wouldn't know that. He must have reached out sometime when the men weren't looking and grabbed the snake from a box of treasure.

ELENA: We should take it to the police. We'll be heroes! And we'll get the reward!

MICHAEL: We can't go to the police yet. We need real evidence first. We don't even know if this is part of the treasure.

ELENA: So how will we find out?

MICHAEL: Tomorrow we'll take the snake to a museum. And then we'll know for sure!

SCENE 5

NARRATOR 2: After school the next day, Michael and Elena walk down the subway platform. They have no idea they are being followed. But a Man with Binoculars is close behind them, watching them on their way to the museum.

NARRATOR 1: As they arrive at the museum and climb the great stone steps, he is still following. And when a man at the information desk points them toward the office of the Director of Mexican Studies, he is still watching.

DIRECTOR: So, what can I do for you today?

MICHAEL: We found an object. It might be a piece of sculpture.

DIRECTOR: Let's have a look at it, then.

NARRATOR 1: Elena hands her the snake and the director studies it closely.

DIRECTOR: Well, what do you know? You've found a Quetzalcoatl. That's quite a find. It's certainly old, probably pre-Columbian.

ELENA: Pre-Columbian?

DIRECTOR: Before Columbus. It's probably Aztec. It's gold and the eyes are jade. Do you know about Quetzalcoatl?

ELENA: No, but the name sounds familiar. I don't know why.

DIRECTOR: The Quetzalcoatl is an ancient Mexican symbol. It represents a god who took the form of a plumed serpent—a feathered snake. The Indians—the Mayas, Toltecs, and Aztecs— used to put it on buildings, in paintings, and in objects like this one. Where did you get it?

MICHAEL: Well, we found it. I mean, a friend of ours found it.

ELENA: In Mexico.

DIRECTOR: I hope your friend reported it, because it's illegal to take artifacts like this out of Mexico. Can you wait here a minute? I'll be right back.

NARRATOR 2: Michael and Elena hear the director using the phone in the next room.

MICHAEL: She doesn't believe us. Let's get out of here!

SCENE 6

NARRATOR 1: They hurry out of the museum and back to the subway. The Man with Binoculars is still following them, though they don't know it. But when Elena opens her pocketbook back at home, they find out one thing they hadn't known.

ELENA: Michael! The golden snake is gone!

MICHAEL: Holding onto the golden snake was the one thing you were supposed to do!

ELENA: But Michael, see how tight that clasp is? It *couldn't* have opened by itself.

MICHAEL: Somebody must have lifted it out of your pocketbook on the subway.

ELENA: But who?

MICHAEL: The only people who might have had any idea we had the snake are the museum director, Big Man, and Blue Jeans.

ELENA: But we would have seen any of them if they were on the subway with us.

MICHAEL: Which means we have no idea who stole the snake. Elena, we could be in real trouble.

ELENA: Why?

MICHAEL: What if the museum director called the police? What if the police trace us here, and we've got no snake? They'll never believe it was stolen. We've got to get into that pet shop and find the rest of the treasure. We'll find it, and then go to the police and prove we're innocent.

ELENA: How are we going to do that?

MICHAEL: Tomorrow afternoon, we'll risk going into the pet shop one more time. Then you'll do something to get Big Man and Blue Jeans's attention so I can run upstairs and look around. Then I'll sneak out onto the fire escape.

ELENA: Okay. I know just what I can do.

NARRATOR 1: So the next day they go back to the pet shop and put Michael's plan into action. They look at the pets for awhile. Then, as Michael moves toward the stairs, Elena opens the latch on the monkey's cage.

BIG MAN: Hey! What are you doing? That monkey is loose! Catch him!

NARRATOR 2: The monkey is screaming, running into things, and swinging on anything that is handy. Finally, the monkey jumps on Big Man's shoulders.

BIG MAN: Get him off me!

NARRATOR 1: Elena gently pulls the monkey off Big Man's shoulders and carries him back to his cage.

BIG MAN: Hey, where'd the boy get to?

ELENA: Oh, my brother ran off. He's afraid of monkeys.

BIG MAN: I never want to see either of you in here again!

NARRATOR 2: Elena leaves the pet shop, returning home to wait by the second-floor window for Michael. What she can't know is that she isn't the only one watching the pet shop's windows. The Man with Binoculars is watching, too.

SCENE 7

PARROT: Catch a cold, catch a cold!

NARRATOR 1: Michael hears the parrot in its cage on the first floor.

MICHAEL: Wait a minute! The parrot's not saying "catch a cold." It's saying, "Quetzalcoatl." Someone here was talking about a Quetzalcoatl, and the parrot picked up the word!

NARRATOR 2: Michael hears the two men working below. He knows he doesn't have much time. He starts searching the crates that the movers have brought in, but doesn't find anything until he reaches the biggest crate in the room.

NARRATOR 1: Michael sees that there is something different about this crate. For one thing, there is a thick panel on the bottom. But why? Michael pulls out his penknife and pries around the edges of the panel.

MICHAEL: Hey! The whole front comes off! There's a drawer inside.

NARRATOR 2: And there is the treasure! The jewels light up the whole room. Michael remembers a description he had once read about the Aztec treasure that said it was "the most lifelike copies of every created thing . . . whether on land or sea, in gold and silver, as well as in precious stones."

NARRATOR 1: Suddenly, Michael is grabbed from behind, and a strong hand covers his mouth.

BLUE JEANS: Don't make a sound.

SCENE 8

NARRATOR 1: Elena has been waiting by the second-floor window for a very long time. It has been almost two hours since she left the pet shop. She is afraid Michael might be in trouble.

NARRATOR 2: Finally, she sees the lights go out in the shop's first-floor windows. Big Man walks out and locks the door behind him. Elena runs out onto the fire escape and puts her face up to the pet shop's second-floor window, but she can't see anything. The window is too dirty.

ELENA: Michael, where are you? Michael, answer me! Are you . . .

NARRATOR 1: Before she can finish her question the window pops open, and Blue Jeans pokes his head out. Michael is standing behind him.

BLUE JEANS: Get in here. And keep quiet.

MICHAEL: It's okay, Elena. Blue Jeans is on our side!

NARRATOR 1: Blue Jeans leads Elena into the storeroom.

BLUE JEANS: Elena, I can explain, but I have to do it fast. The smuggler just went to meet his art dealer. They'll be back here any minute. I'm Joe Bowler, a U.S. Customs Department agent. I've been on their trail for weeks. I finally got myself a job where I could keep an eye on them. I didn't want to arrest them until we could find out who's buying the stuff, and just where it's coming from.

NARRATOR 2: Suddenly, they hear the downstairs door open.

BLUE JEANS: I'll close the crate and hide on the other side of the room. Stay here and don't make a sound!

NARRATOR 1: Michael and Elena hear two men enter the room. They recognize one of the voices as Big Man's.

BIG MAN: This is the biggest haul we've brought in so far, Mr. Kane. I'm sure you'll find everything to your liking. Everything is solid gold.

NARRATOR 2: Big Man opens the crate full of treasure.

BIG MAN: So, do you like what you see?

KANE: Beautiful! Where'd you get this stuff?

BIG MAN: That's my secret.

KANE: Hey, I just want to make sure it's authentic Aztec stuff.

BIG MAN: You know the stuff's real. Now what's your offer? I was thinking in the neighborhood of $50,000 for the whole lot; $75,000 if I throw in this special item.

NARRATOR 1: Big Man pulls out another plumed serpent—a Quetzalcoatl. This one is much larger than the one Elena had found.

BIG MAN: So, are you interested? Hey! Who left that window open?

NARRATOR 2: Suddenly, Blue Jeans jumps out from behind a crate.

BLUE JEANS: Stay where you are! You're both under arrest!

BIG MAN: You're not arresting me, you double-crosser!

NARRATOR 1: Big Man takes a swing at Blue Jeans, who jumps out of the way and hits Big Man. Blue Jeans would have ended the fight quickly if Mr. Kane hadn't snuck up behind him with the Quetzalcoatl.

ELENA: Look out!

NARRATOR 2: But it's too late. Blue Jeans is knocked out with the statue, and Elena has given up her and Michael's hiding place.

NARRATOR 1: Big Man and Mr. Kane move toward Michael and Elena, but Big Man stumbles and accidentally knocks over one of the snake tanks.

NARRATOR 2: The men see the six-foot boa constrictor and head toward the stairs. Michael and Elena chase after them, each pushing a heavy crate. And down go Big Man and Mr. Kane! They tumble down the stairs, crying in pain. Then there is the sound of police sirens.

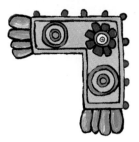

SCENE 9

NARRATOR 1: And just like that, it is all over. The police make the arrests, gather up the treasure, and close the pet shop.

NARRATOR 2: Then Blue Jeans brings Michael and Elena home. Mama and Grandma are worried sick about them, because they are late for dinner. But Officer Bowler explains everything.

ELENA: So whatever happened to my gold snake?

BLUE JEANS: As soon as I knew you were on to something, I telephoned my partner to tail you. He followed you into the museum. We were afraid you'd give the whole thing away before we were ready, so he took the Quetzalcoatl while you were on the subway.

ELENA: But how did you know Michael was in the storeroom?

BLUE JEANS: My partner was watching the shop with his binoculars, waiting for the smuggler to arrive with the art dealer. He saw you both go into the store, but only one of you came out. When the smuggler left, he contacted me on my walkie-talkie. That's when I grabbed you, Michael.

MICHAEL: And so your partner called the police.

BLUE JEANS: That's right. But what's the matter, kid? You look down. I'd think you'd be happy.

MICHAEL: Well, I was just thinking about the reward. You were working on the case first, so I guess you get the money.

BLUE JEANS: Hey, you kids found the first piece of the treasure. Besides, government agents don't get rewards. I think we can convince the Mexican government that they owe you the $5,000.

NARRATOR 1: So the mystery is solved. Michael and Elena got the reward, along with a free vacation in Mexico, courtesy of the Mexican government.

NARRATOR 2: And Number 22 is empty, again. But things change.

How to
Create a
Visual Mystery

Many different things are happening at once.

When detectives—or forensic scientists, such as Lilly Gallman—go to the scene of an accident or a crime, they must observe every detail in order to figure out what really happened. Junior detectives can sharpen their powers of observation by studying a visual mystery.

What is a visual mystery? A visual mystery includes a detailed picture of a crime scene, an accident scene, or any type of action scene. Like a real-life investigator at the scene of a crime, the "investigator" of a visual mystery must study the picture, then note details, make inferences, and draw conclusions.

Questions like this require the reader to draw conclusions from several details.

SCENE OF THE ACCIDENT

You were witness to an auto collision, and a bicycle accident. The police would like your firsthand account of what happened. Cover up the picture of the street scene and answer the following questions to the best of your memory.

1. Approximately what time was it?
2. How many onlookers were standing in the intersection after the collision?
3. What was the license number of the car in the foreground?
4. How many people were in the car?
5. What traffic law had the driver broken?
6. What movie was playing at the theater?
7. Above what store was the fire?
8. What sign was posted at the open manhole?

Even the smallest details might be important!

The questions ask for many different types of information.

Signs, as well as pictures, are included.

1 Brainstorm for Ideas

Think about where you would like your visual mystery to be set. The setting might be a busy city street, such as the one in the example. It also could be some other crowded place, such as a concert or a sporting event. Maybe you'd like to create a really funny, or scary, scene. No matter what your scene is like, it should contain plenty of action and lots of details!

TOOLS

- Paper and pencil

- Drawing paper, markers, and other art supplies

- Magazines and newspapers (optional)

Tip You'll probably want your scene to include text, as well as pictures. Clip pictures that contain written information, or add words to the scene by hand.

2 Create Your Scene

Put together a scene for your visual mystery. You may want to draw the entire scene. (Be sure that the things you draw are easy to identify.) Otherwise, you can create your scene by using pictures cut out from old magazines and newspapers. Old postcards are also good resources. Use one full-page picture, or cut out several smaller pictures and paste them together on a piece of construction paper or posterboard. You can also create your scene by combining drawings and cutouts.

3 Write Questions

Write a list of questions to accompany your scene. You'll probably want to write about 10 to 12 questions. Examine your scene carefully before you begin to write. Think of some questions about important details, as well as a few about really small details.

Some of your questions may require the viewer to make inferences and draw conclusions. But each question should have a single clear-cut answer. Don't ask questions that could have more than one correct answer.

Write an answer key to hand out to classmates who try your visual mystery. Making the key will also help you to be sure that each question has one clear-cut answer.

If You Are Using a Computer . . .

Browse through the collection of clip art on your computer to find illustrations for your Visual Mystery. Use the Journal format to draft your Visual Mystery questions.

4 Share Your Mystery

Swap visual mysteries with a partner. Study each other's scene, and try to answer each other's questions. (Have your partner write her or his answers on a separate sheet of paper so that you can trade questions with others later.) Just for fun, give yourself one point for every one of your partner's questions that you answer correctly. Give yourself an additional point for every one of your questions that stumps your partner. Have your partner use the same scoring system. Compare scores. How did you do?

THINK

How can being a careful observer help you in your everyday life?

Lilly Gallman
Forensic Chemist ▶

Analyzing clues and evidence
helps us solve mysteries.

Looking for Clues

Follow the trail of
the Bloodhound
Gang as they crack
a puzzling case.

Read about
some important
breakthroughs in
crime detection.

Meet forensic
chemist Lilly
Gallman, who
uses science to
help solve crimes.

WORKSHOP 2

Write a mini-mystery that will
baffle your friends.

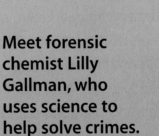

The Case of the
Buried Treasure

"From the gleam in your eye, I deduce you are about to
get rich quick," said Dr. Haledjian.
"Clever of you, old chap," said Bertie Tilford, a young
Englishman with a superiority complex toward work. "If
I had a mere ten thousand I should realize a fortune!
Have you ten?"
"What's the game now?" demanded Haledjian. "Pieces
of eight among the corals? Doubloons from Kidd's

from

The Case
of the
SECRET MESSAGE

BY **SID FLEISCHMAN**
ILLUSTRATED BY **KEN BARR**

Vikki was running.

At this hour of the morning the green strip of park along the river had the look of an outdoor gymnasium. Joggers and runners charged along in broken file. Others leaned against tree trunks to stretch and limber up.

Vikki wanted to get in five miles before going to work. She wore running shorts trimmed in orange and a white T-shirt. In black letters across the back it read:

BLOODHOUND DETECTIVE AGENCY

Whenever there's trouble,
we're there on the double.

She maintained a steady long-legged stride. At sixteen, she was taller than most of the boys her age. If she had once felt awkward and self-conscious about it, she now dismissed the matter with a snap of her fingers. She couldn't bother her head with things beyond her control. And she now regarded it as childish to base friendships on feet and inches.

Still, she couldn't help noticing that the boys were beginning to catch up fast. Especially Ricardo, who was a year younger and already as tall as she. The third member of the Bloodhound Gang didn't count. Zach was only ten.

She had tried to get them to run with her, but Ricardo preferred to sleep in. And Zach saw no point in running—unless someone was chasing him.

She had covered almost three miles. Squirrels scattered from her path and birds darted through the trees. A familiar voice broke through the sound of her breathing.

"Hey—Bloodhound!"

She saw Ricardo farther along the path. He had set up his tripod and camera mounted with a telephoto lens.

"Has there been an earthquake?" Vikki shouted.

"No, why?"

"I can't think of anything else that would get you out of bed this early."

"Any sacrifice for my art," Ricardo remarked airily. He too was wearing an office T-shirt, a gift from Mr. Bloodhound to the Bloodhound Gang. "I thought Mr. B. would like a picture of his running billboard."

"Well, I'm not going to break stride to pose."

"Who asked you to? I want an action shot. Keep running. I'll focus on your back."

She passed him by. After a moment she heard the faint clicks of the camera.

She was hardly aware of the shabby woman in old shoes with run-down heels on the path ahead. But quite suddenly a man appeared from behind a tree, as if waiting in ambush. He rushed up behind the old woman.

"Hey!" Vikki yelled.

In a flash the man ripped the old lady's handbag from her grasp and took off. The gray-haired woman set up a wail and tried to run after him.

"Stop! Thief!"

The purse snatcher was cutting across the park toward the street and the early morning traffic. The old lady could do little more than hobble along in her run-down heels.

Vikki turned to shout back at Ricardo. "A purse snatcher! Come on!"

In a matter of seconds Vikki caught up with the woman.

"Bloodhound Detective Agency! We'll catch him!"

She raced across the lawn after the thief. Ricardo gathered up the tripod, threw it against his shoulder, and followed. But the camera equipment slowed him down.

The thief darted through the trees, never looking back. All Vikki could see

of him was faded jeans, a faded blue sweatshirt, and a neck as long and as scrawny as a plucked chicken's.

When he reached the street he barely paused for traffic. Vikki hesitated, waving Ricardo on. Then she crossed and poured on a burst of speed.

The thief sprinted along the empty sidewalk. His ears had turned red as tomatoes. A flat-footed running style, Vikki noticed. He was getting winded.

"Purse snatcher! Stop him!" she yelled out.

He turned his head with a look of surprise that he hadn't shaken her.

Ricardo hadn't crossed the street; he had gained some distance by following the edge of the park.

The purse snatcher ducked down a narrow side street lined with parked cars and trash cans. He looked back again. The long-legged girl was gaining on him. His face was flushed. He hesitated—and then tossed the purse into a trash can.

That stopped Vikki.

"Hey, punk!" she shouted. "Ripping off an old lady—that sure took guts!"

The thief, loping away, tossed back a weary frown. Unheard, a camera shutter tripped open and shut. Ricardo had jammed the tripod in the grass and focused down the narrow street. He had caught the purse snatcher on film.

Vikki dug into the trash can and plucked out the old black handbag. She was glad to see the clasp still closed. The sneak thief hadn't had time to paw through it.

Once again Ricardo gathered up the tripod. He crossed the street and met Vikki at the corner.

"I got him," Ricardo said. "Full face shot."

"Terrific," Vikki gasped. For the first time she realized she was out of breath. "Now, where's the old lady?"

"She was somewhere behind me."

They glanced back across the street to the park. The gray-haired woman, wearing steel-rimmed glasses and a long, shapeless old sweater, was waving to them.

Then a dark limousine pulled up beside her. Two men leaped out the doors, grabbed the woman roughly, and pitched her into the car. The doors slammed, the engine revved up, and the limousine sped away.

Vikki's eyebrows took a leap. "Hey!"

"She's being kidnapped!" exclaimed Ricardo.

"Get the license!"

"Got it."

"Me too."

The license plate read: MR. BIG.

 The young detectives returned to the upstairs office of the Bloodhound Detective Agency.

Ricardo called the police and reported everything that had just happened.

Vikki opened the black handbag and shook the contents onto the desk. A plain white envelope fell out.

"What else is there?" Ricardo asked.

"That's all there is," Vikki said.

"Just an envelope? There ought to be some identification."

Vikki nodded. "Ought to be, but isn't." She turned the purse inside out. She felt the sides in the event something was concealed in the lining. Nothing.

Ricardo picked up the envelope. "Blank."

"I can see that. And sealed."

Ricardo held the envelope up to the sunlight streaming through the window. "There's something inside. A letter, I guess."

"Think we ought to open it?" Vikki asked.

"It may be addressed to that old lady."

"There's no stamp. So it wouldn't be exactly as if we were opening someone's mail."

"Right," said Ricardo. Carefully he began to peel open the sealed flap.

At that moment the door opened and Zach came gliding in on his skateboard. He saw that Vikki was in shorts. "What happened? Did your pants shrink up?"

"Wise guy," Vikki said with a distracted air. "Zach, get on the radio. See if you can turn up any information on a Mr. Big."

"Mr. Big? What kind of case are we on?"

"Let's just say it looks like a *big* one."

Zach ambled over to the CB radio, snapped it on, and picked up the microphone. "Breaker one-two, breaker one-two . . ." he said.

Ricardo withdrew a folded sheet of white paper from the envelope. He opened it up.

"Blank, Vikki. Both sides."

For a moment their eyes met in baffled wonder. "It doesn't add up," Vikki said finally. "Why would a woman walk around with nothing in her purse but this? A blank sheet of paper sealed up in a blank envelope?"

"It must add up to something," Ricardo answered. "Why would those guys kidnap a shabby old lady?"

Vikki snapped her fingers. "Maybe it wasn't the old lady they were after. Maybe it was this blank piece of paper."

"Secret writing?"

Vikki nodded. "Secret writing. Must be. I'm going to call Mr. Bloodhound. He knows all about that stuff."

While she dialed the phone, Ricardo snapped on the desk lamp and heated the paper against the light bulb.

Zach's voice droned on. "Breaker one-two. Doesn't anyone have their ears on? This is Private Eye."

A voice erupted from the CB radio. "Go ahead, breaker."

"This is Private Eye looking for an I.D. on a Mr. Big. Any info, you guys? Give me a holler."

Vikki turned from the phone. "Thanks, Mr. Bloodhound. Hang on a minute." She caught Ricardo's attention. "He says if the invisible writing was done with lemon juice, heat will bring it out."

"I know that one," Ricardo replied. "But it's not working. Or this blank paper really *is* blank."

Into the phone Vikki said, "It must not be lemon juice, Mr. Bloodhound. Is there anything else we can try?. . . Salt water? I'll call you back if that doesn't work."

She took the sheet of paper from Ricardo and laid it flat on the desk. Then she pulled open a drawer and chose a pencil. She tested the lead for softness.

"That ought to do it," she declared.

"Do what?"

"Mr. Bloodhound says you can write secret messages with strong salt water. The writing appears when you scribble with a soft pencil."

She laid the pencil point almost on its side and began shading in the left side of the sheet with long strokes.

"See anything?" Ricardo muttered.

"Don't get anxious."

"I *am* anxious."

"I sure hope the police find the old lady," said Vikki, scribbling away.

"We reported it right away, didn't we? They ought to be able to trace the license. Unless it's a phony."

"The purse snatcher was no phony."

"I'll develop the film and hand a print over to the cops. That ought to cure him of grabbing purses. I caught him full face with the telephoto lens."

A ghostly image was beginning to form through the pencil strokes on the paper.

"See that?" asked Vikki. She felt a quick surge of excitement. There *was* a message.

"You've hit it. Keep going."

"It looks like the number ten." Vikki had to stop to sharpen the pencil. Then, hurrying, she shaded in the rest of the page. Faintly, the balance of the secret message appeared.

 Vikki and Ricardo gazed at the coded message.

"Can you make any sense out of it?" she murmured.

"Ten . . . S . . . E . . . Ten . . . S . . . E. Beats me. It's going to take time to break the code, Vikki."

"I'll think about it in the shower. I've got to dash home and change. I won't be long."

Vikki returned in less than half an hour, wearing jeans and a pumpkin-colored turtleneck. Zach was still at the CB radio. And Ricardo was studying the message intensely, as if it were a school test.

"I think I've got part of it," he said, looking up. "Ten . . . S . . . E. It could be a direction. Ten southeast."

Zach turned suddenly from the radio.

"Sounds like Tennessee to me."

"What does?" Vikki asked.

"Ten . . . S . . . E. Tenn-ess-ee."

"Hey—I think you've got it!" Ricardo blurted out. "What took you so long? Sure, Tennessee!"

Vikki looked puzzled. "Tennessee Bay? Is there a place like that around here?"

"Never heard of it," said Ricardo.

Vikki crossed to a wooden cabinet and rummaged around. She withdrew a large rolled-up area map and spread it on the floor. "Let's start looking," she said.

Zach began to take quick notes as a fast-talking voice broke in on the CB. Finally Zach said, "Thanks for the comeback, Invisible Man. This is Private Eye wishing good numbers on you."

He leaped up to face Vikki and Ricardo.

"Got it! Guess who Mr. Big is? A big-time smuggler. Yeah, runs a smuggling ring. Dangerous. His real name is Aces."

"Smuggles what?" Vikki asked.

"Jewels. Stolen stuff, I guess."

"Tennessee Bay," Ricardo said. "Do you suppose—"

The phone rang.

Vikki snapped up the receiver. "Bloodhound Detective Agency," she said hastily. "Whenever there's trouble, we're there on the double. Mr. Bloodhound isn't here. Victoria Allen speaking."

She fell silent, listening, then looked darkly at Ricardo and Zach. Finally, taking a deep breath, she muttered, "Yes, sir. We'll expect you, Mr. Aces." She hung up.

Ricardo and Zach gave her wide-eyed looks.

"Mr. Aces?" Ricardo whispered. "Mr. Big in person?"

"He claims to be that old lady's nephew. He's coming right over. For the purse."

"Gulp," Ricardo said.

Vikki shrugged off a sense of impending danger. "Let's roll up the map and duck it out of sight. We'll seal another piece of paper in the envelope."

The Bloodhound Gang went into action. Zach returned the map to the cabinet. Vikki used office paste to reseal the envelope and stuffed it back inside the purse.

"What'll I do with the real message?" Ricardo asked.

"Just hide it!"

There came a knock at the door. The Bloodhound Gang froze, barely exchanging glances.

"Mr. Big . . ." Vikki whispered.

Ricardo swallowed hard. "He sure got here fast." In a slight panic, he looked for a place to hide the exposed message. Then he crushed it into a ball and poked it into the mouth of a skull yellowed with age

that was sitting among the relics of Mr. Bloodhound's cases.

"Come in," Vikki called out.

The door opened.

The shabby gray-haired woman in run-down heels walked in.

"Ah, there you are, my dear," she said, recognizing Vikki. "What a courageous young lady!"

Vikki was caught almost speechless. "But-but . . ."

"I'm Mrs. Frimple," said the old woman, adjusting her steel-rimmed glasses. "And I see you recovered my purse from that scamp."

"But, Mrs. Frimple, you were *kidnapped!*" Vikki exclaimed.

"Me? My stars, what gave you that idea?"

"But I saw . . ."

"Who'd want to abduct me? No, no, my dear. Mrs. Frimple is just fine—never better."

She smiled, picked up her purse, and returned to the door.

"Thank you, my dears. All of you."

And she was gone.

Ricardo shook his head in stunned bafflement. "Did you just see what I just saw?"

"She's putting us on," said Vikki, after a moment's thought. "Her story's fishy. She escaped. And she came back for the message."

Zach gave a small whistle. "Wait till she discovers you slipped her a blank piece of paper!"

Mr. Big didn't bother to knock.

He filled the doorway, a stout man with pale blue eyes. His double chins had double chins. He was carrying a gold-handled walking stick. Once through the doorway, he was followed by a bodyguard with a squashed nose and hands in leather gloves.

Mr. Big raised the walking stick like an overweight fencer and pointed at Vikki.

"Let's have it," he growled.

"Have what?" Vikki tried to smile. "Do you have an appointment?"

Mr. Big glanced at his bodyguard. "Knuckles, give 'em my card."

"Which one, boss?"

"Pick any one!"

The bodyguard dug through his pockets and came up with an assortment of business cards. He began shuffling through them. "How about Ace Reducing Saloon?"

"That's 'Salon,' stupid."

The bodyguard kept shuffling through the cards. "Ace Exterminating Company, Ace Jewelry Corporation, Ace Model Airplanes . . ."

"Never mind," Vikki remarked. "You must be Mr. Ace."

"Mr. Aces," the heavy man corrected her. "Hand over the purse."

Vikki was doing her best to play it cool. "How is your aunt?"

"All shook up. Can't leave her room. Come on, kid. I'm in a hurry."

"I'm sorry, Mr. Aces. We don't have the purse."

Mr. Big waved his cane in the air. "Don't give me that! Anything happens on the streets and I get the word. Fast. You got the purse."

"*Had* it," Ricardo put in.

"Mrs. Frimple picked it up about ten minutes ago," said Vikki.

Mr. Big's face reddened with anger. He flashed a hard look at Knuckles.

"You told me the old lady was—"

"These punks are lying, boss."

Mr. Big sliced the air with his walking stick. "Then tear this place apart. Find it!"

The cane swept a shelf, accidentally knocking the skull to the floor. A crumpled piece of paper flew out of its mouth. Mr. Big spied it with his sharp little eyes.

"Well, well, what have we here?"

The Bloodhound Gang held its breath.

"Oh, that," said Ricardo an instant later. "Just trash, sir. We use that old skull for a wastebasket." He bent down to retrieve the wad of paper.

But the tip of Mr. Big's walking stick got there first. Using the cane like a golf club, he putted the ball of paper toward his bodyguard's feet.

"Pick it up, Knuckles."

"Right, boss."

"Now hand it to me."

A moment later Mr. Big had opened the crumpled paper. After a quick look, he stuffed the message in his pocket and peeped at the Bloodhound Gang. The cold blink of his eyelids gave Vikki a quick chill.

Knuckles tugged at his leather gloves. "Want me to take care of 'em, boss?"

Mr. Big shook his head. "Naw—just a bunch of numbers. And a bunch of kids. What do they know? Come on."

He led Knuckles to the door. He stopped and turned for a final look at the Bloodhound Gang.

"Forget about all this, understand? Unless you'd like Knuckles here to fit you for new shoes."

"Shoes?" Zach muttered.

"Cement shoes. Courtesy of Ace Cement Company. And a swim in the river. Courtesy of Ace Funeral Homes. Get it?"

"Got it," Vikki muttered. And then she added with a mocking smile, "Have a nice day."

 "Have a nice day?" Ricardo groaned. "His idea of a nice day is to visit the morgue."

"Oh, he's a pussycat," Vikki said, turning to the cabinet.

"A pussycat with claws like meat hooks."

Vikki withdrew the map. "Now, where were we?"

"Didn't you hear what he said?" Zach put in. "He said *forget* it."

"We don't take orders from cheap hoodlums."

"How about expensive ones?" Ricardo remarked. "He's got more businesses than the yellow pages."

"Ah, here it is," Vikki exclaimed, her fingertip on the map. "Tennessee Bay. Looks about thirty miles south of here. Now what were the rest of those numbers?"

"Vikki, I think we ought to turn this case over to Mr. Bloodhound," Zach persisted.

Ricardo gave a defiant shrug. "Naw. *We're* detectives, aren't we? Vikki's right. Let's get on with it. A crook is a crook."

"And a code is a code," Vikki said. "We'll call Mr. Bloodhound when we break it."

"Eight," Ricardo said.

"What?" asked Vikki, as if his mind had begun to wander.

"The next line of the message. It started with an eight."

Vikki snapped her fingers. "Of course. Right. Eight twenty-five."

"Sounds like the time," said Ricardo.

Vikki sat at the desk and picked up a pencil. "But it had a slant in the middle. Like this." On a pad she wrote:

8/25

"Got it!" Ricardo exclaimed. "That's the way you write a date."

"Eight twenty-five." Vikki looked up. "Hey—that's today's date. August twenty-fifth."

Ricardo smiled. "That explains it."

"Explains *what*?" asked Zach.

"Why Mrs. Frimple and Mr. Big were in such a hurry to lay their hands on the message. Some crime is going to happen—today."

Vikki gave a quick nod and held the pencil poised over the note pad. She searched her memory for the last set of numbers in the message.

"Got it," she muttered, and jotted down four numbers.

1930

"Nineteen-thirty," Ricardo said, reading the pad upside down. "If that's the year, the crime was committed more than fifty years ago. Doesn't make sense."

Vikki leaned back in the desk chair. "It can't be the year. Let's think it through. If you were planning a crime, and sending a message, what would you write? The place . . ."

"We've got that," said Ricardo.

"The day . . ."

"We've got that."

"The hour . . ."

"That we *don't* have," Ricardo declared.

"Boy, are you guys dumb!" Zach joined in. "That's the way they tell time on ships and stuff."

"What is?" asked Vikki.

"With numbers like nineteen-thirty."

"Great, Zach. But what time does it make?"

Zach began to enjoy being one-up on Vikki and Ricardo. "You don't start over again at noon. One o'clock is thirteen hundred hours. Two o'clock is fourteen hundred hours. And so on."

Ricardo picked up on the system. "Then you subtract twelve noon from nineteen-thirty—"

"And get seven-thirty. Seven-thirty *tonight*."

She grabbed the phone and dialed. After a moment she said, "Hello, Mrs. Bloodhound. We're onto a case that might interest Mr. Bloodhound. What? . . . Oh . . . Well, never mind. We can handle it. No, there's no danger. But we're going to have to raid the office petty-cash box for bus fare."

All eyes were on her as Vikki hung up. She gave Ricardo and Zach an unruffled smile. "Mr. B. had to catch a plane. Looks like we're on our own."

Ricardo winked reassuringly, inflated his cheeks, and mimicked Mr. Big.

"A bunch of kids. What do they know?"

"What we don't know is exactly what's going to happen tonight," said Vikki.

Zach mused aloud. "Ships . . ."

"And smuggling," Ricardo added.

"Must be it," Vikki nodded. "At Tennessee Bay!"

 It was late afternoon when the Bloodhound Gang boarded a southbound bus out of the central station.

By then Ricardo had developed the roll of film shot that morning in the park. He had brought along the prints, still slightly damp, and passed them around.

"Check out this shot of the back of your T-shirt."

"Right on. The letters are razor sharp."

"But look, Vikki. You can make out Mrs. Frimple ahead of you on the path. Of course, she's a little out of focus."

Vikki studied the picture carefully. "I'd say she's out of focus in more ways than one. She's not one of your run-of-the-mill little old ladies. Escaped from Mr. Big's goons like a regular Houdini. And then tried to make us believe she'd never been kidnapped at all."

"Yeah, she's mixed up in this caper somehow."

Then Ricardo handed over a close-up of the purse snatcher. "How's that for a mug shot?"

"The police will love it," Vikki replied. "Look at all those gaps between his teeth. Like a picket fence. He's practically behind bars."

"What time is it?" Zach asked.

Vikki glanced at her watch and did a moment's figuring. "Almost sixteen-thirty hours."

"We're going to be awfully early."

"That's the idea," said Vikki. "To get there long before Mr. Big, settle in, and wait."

Ricardo, burdened with his camera bag, nodded. "He's bound to be careful not to be followed. But we'll be way ahead of him."

The city receded block by block, and after a while the bus began working its way through the beach towns. Zach, who had never been this way before, kept shifting his gaze from the side windows to the broader back windows. That way, the sights didn't zip by so quickly.

"Ricardo," Vikki said, "think you'll have enough light to grab pictures of whatever is going to happen?"

"Plenty. If the smugglers are on time. But just in case, I loaded the camera with fast film."

Zach shifted his eyes from the rear window. "You know how in movies someone jumps in a taxi and says 'Follow that car'?"

"Yeah," Ricardo answered with complete disinterest.

"Have you ever heard anyone say 'Follow that bus'?"

"What are you talking about?"

"There's a tan car tailing this bus."

Vikki and Ricardo spun around to peer out through the back window.

"See it?" Zach asked. "Following about a block behind. I think it's been trailing along ever since we left town."

"Looks like two people in the front seat," Vikki said. "Can you make them out? Wish we had binoculars."

"We don't need binoculars." Quickly Ricardo dug the camera out of his bag and set about changing lenses.

"What are you doing?" Vikki asked.

"Putting the telephoto back on. I can zoom them up almost close enough to touch."

He aimed the camera through the window and carefully turned the barrel of the lens. Then he stopped, squinting through the viewer with one eye. He let out a slow whistle.

"Do we know them?" Vikki asked.

"The man at the wheel—never saw him before. But guess who's sitting beside him?"

"Let's skip the guessing games, Ricky," Vikki said. "Who?"

"Yup. There she is, all right. In perfect focus."

"*Who*?"

"Mrs. Frimple."

 Ricardo arched an eyebrow. "How are we going to give her the slip in broad daylight?"

The bus made another stop to let passengers off and on.

"Maybe we can fake her out," Vikki said, rising. "Come on. We'll walk down the aisle as if we were getting off."

The Bloodhound Gang rose, but partway down the aisle Vikki motioned to duck down and keep out of sight. Scurrying like crabs, the three detectives returned to the back-seat area. The other passengers turned their heads, but Vikki couldn't concern herself with their puzzled stares.

The Bloodhound Gang remained slumped out of sight from the rear window through several more stops. At one point the bus driver motioned a car to pass on the narrow road. Vikki dug out her pocket mirror and caught a glimpse of the car.

"Tan car?" Zach asked.

"You guessed it," Vikki answered. "They must be checking the passengers for us as they drive past the bus. Stay down. They'll be turning back if they figure we managed to slip out at an earlier stop."

It was almost half an hour before the bus approached Tennessee Bay. Ricardo rose slowly and risked a backward glance.

"All clear." He smiled. "Vikki, we sure gave them a lot of busy-work. Now they're doubling back on our trail."

Vikki replied with a playful smile, "Why, I just feel terrible about it!"

The Bloodhound Gang straightened up. The bus was slowing. A road sign announced:

TENNESSEE BAY CITY
Population 47

"A regular boom town," Ricardo said.

The bus pulled into the city—a gas station, a grocery store, a café, and a shack with a "For Rent" sign in the window.

No one got off the bus—except the Bloodhound Gang.

The bay was a mud flat about a mile across. It had an abandoned look, as if the tide had gone out and forgotten to come back.

The Bloodhound Gang scouted along a dirt road and then cut off into a patch of tall, dry grass to hide. And wait.

Peering through the telephoto lens, Ricardo began studying the mud flat and the ocean beyond.

"What time is it?" Zach asked. "I'm getting hungry."

Vikki checked her watch. "It's . . . seventeen-twenty hours."

"We should have stopped in that café for something to eat," Zach said.

"That's about the first place Mrs. Frimple would ask about us."

Ricardo lowered the camera. "Vikki, I think we're in the wrong place."

"You like the grass over there better?"

"This bay is so shallow, you'd have to dig to find water. Smugglers couldn't even get a rowboat across."

Vikki shook her head. "This has *got* to be the right place."

Twenty minutes later they suddenly heard a rustling in the weeds behind them.

"Looks cozy," came a voice. "Is there room for one more? And anyone hungry?"

The voice was young and joyous. The figure was old and familiar.

"Mrs. Frimple," Vikki gasped.

"Not exactly." The woman set down a wooden box and a grocery bag. Then she whipped off a gray wig and shook out her own honey-colored hair. She pulled off the steel-rimmed glasses and unbuttoned the shabby sweater to reveal a police badge.

"Police Detective Monroe," she declared, and smiled. "How do I look?"

"Fifty years younger," said Vikki.

"How'd you find us?" Zach blurted out.

"My partner and I figured you'd spotted us. So we drove on ahead.

I took the wheel and he got out and caught the bus. He saw you get off here at Tennessee Bay. Once you were out of sight, he left the bus too—and then flagged me down. I'd have been here sooner, but I stopped to have some sandwiches made up. You have your choice of ham and cheese, tuna fish, peanut butter, or egg salad."

"Peanut butter," Zach said quickly, while there was still a choice.

"But why were you shadowing us?" Ricardo exclaimed.

The police officer grinned. "If you were clever enough to switch the message, I figured you'd be clever enough to lead us to the secret location."

"How did you happen to have the message in the first place?" Vikki asked.

"I worked myself into Mr. Big's organization. Undercover. I got lucky and was able to intercept the message. Somehow they got wise and came after me. That's when the creep in the park snatched my purse. But you came along in the nick of time."

"Speaking of the creep," Ricardo said, "here's a picture of him."

Detective Monroe glanced at the photograph and her eyes lit up. "Rembrandt couldn't have done better. Terrific. We'll pick him up right away."

"But why did you come to the office and deny you'd been kidnapped?" Vikki asked.

"For your own good. I thought once I had the message back, you'd be better off out of the case. But when the message you slipped me turned up blank, I knew you'd broken the code. And I practically ran into Mr. Big as I left your building. So I knew you were in danger. It was then my partner and I decided to keep an eye on you."

"How did you escape from his goons?" Zach put in.

Detective Monroe laughed. "Who expects judo chops from a little old lady?"

"Seems like you should have shadowed Mr. Big instead of us," Ricardo said.

"Oh, we've tried that. A man like Mr. Big grows eyes in the back of his head. Every time we put a tail on him, he leads us on a wild-goose chase. But we've got a chance to catch him red-handed this time. My partner is staked out up the road. What time is the boat due?"

"In a couple of hours . . . seven-thirty—I mean, nineteen-thirty hours," Ricardo replied. "But look at that mud. No boat could get through that."

"Just the sort of spot these smugglers always pick out. We've known for some time that Mr. Big's interest in model airplanes is just a front. His Ace Model Airplane shop always has a 'Closed' sign on it." She pointed to the wooden box she'd carried into the grass. "Exactly why I brought that along. Now, let's eat."

The waiting was over.

At 1923 hours a fishing boat nosed into view outside the bay.

"It's dropping anchor," Ricardo said, zooming the camera lens in on it.

"Can you make out its name?" Detective Monroe asked.

Ricardo squinted at the lettering along the bow. He snapped a picture and rewound the camera. *The Flying Ace.*

"Mr. Big has more aces up his sleeve than a cardsharp," said Detective Monroe, opening up the wooden case. "We'd like any film you shoot. It'll look good in court."

She withdrew a set of earphones from her bag. The box she had brought contained a radio receiver and transmitter.

Moments later Zach exclaimed, "Hey—listen!"

A distant whine floated in the air, sounding like an angry hornet approaching from the sea.

It was exactly 1930 hours.

Quickly the whine became a popping roar as it drew nearer.

"It's coming in over the mud flat," Vikki exclaimed. "Over there! I can see it."

"So can I," said Ricardo, trying to focus his camera. "A model airplane . . . with a gas-powered motor."

"And radio-controlled," added Detective Monroe, slipping on the earphones. "Now all I've got to do is find the radio frequency they're using to guide the plane."

"It's landing at the other end of the bay," Zach declared, pointing through the grass.

"Here comes another one!" said Ricardo, panning his camera back toward the fishing boat.

Detective Monroe, rotating the dials on the receiver, broke into a sudden smile. "Got their frequency. Now to beam our own signal."

She set the dials on the transmitter. "Can you see that second plane?"

"I'm right on it," Ricardo answered, peering through the camera.

"Anything happening?"

Ricardo was hardly breathing. Then he said, "It's turning this way. Coming right for us!"

"Terrific." The police officer was smiling. "Now it's following *our* radio signal."

"And coming in for a landing!" Zach added.

The model airplane roared in low over the mud flat and touched down roughly. It bounced along the ground and disappeared into a clump of grass.

The Bloodhound Gang and Detective Monroe left their hiding place and chased down the plane. It seemed to have disappeared. The motor had stalled out.

Zach dove through the grass and reappeared with the model plane in his hand.

"It's a B-52," he said.

"Never mind what it is," Vikki declared. "Is there something in it?"

"There must be," said Detective Monroe. "Smuggled goods launched from the fishing boat out there. I'll radio the Coast Guard as soon as we know what we've got."

"What we've got," said Vikki, discovering a silk pouch taped inside the plane's cargo hatch, "is something very small." She opened the pouch and poured the contents into her hand for all to see. "Diamonds."

A dark limousine came crashing through the weeds and screeched to a halt. The doors flew open, and out jumped Knuckles. He spread his big hands out like claws.

"Don't move!" he commanded.

Then Mr. Big appeared through the cloud of dust raised by the car's sudden stop. He planted his feet far apart and smiled.

"Hijacking model airplanes," he said, "Tsk tsk, tsk."

And Detective Monroe replied, "Smuggling diamonds. Tsk, tsk, tsk. Sir, you are under arrest."

Mr. Big laughed. "Says who?"

Another figure took shape through the dust, a solidly built man who dropped Knuckles with a karate chop.

"Says me," he said. "Detective Flint. And now for a little police jewelry. Hands behind your back, Mr. Big, unless you want to hear bird song like your pal Knuckles."

By 1944 hours the two criminals were fitted out with gleaming police jewelry—handcuffs.

"Thanks for the assist, Bloodhound Gang," said Detective Monroe. "Good work. Super. Terrific. I'd say everything came up... Aces."

From Police Lab:
Using Science to Solve Crimes

POINTING
★
A FINGER

By Robert Sheely

INKED PRINT

LATENT PRINT

New York City, 1911. "We went to a show that night," the woman said, her voice steady. "Then we went home and to bed. My husband never left the house until the next morning. So there's no way he could have committed the burglary."

The woman peered out from the witness stand. Her eyes met her husband's eyes. He smiled faintly and nodded once, sitting quietly in the courtroom while his wife testified. His name was Caesar Cella. He was a notorious thief with a long record of burglaries in New York City.

On the night Mrs. Cella described, a shop in the heart of the city had been broken into. Unfortunately for the police, there were no eyewitnesses to the burglary. In fact, the only people to testify were five witnesses who swore they had been with Cella and his wife at the show that night.

"Are you absolutely certain, ma'am?" the prosecutor asked Mrs. Cella. As he had done with each of the other witnesses, the prosecutor tried his best to get her to change her story. But it was no use. She stuck by everything she had said. One look at the judge's grim face and the prosecutor knew he was losing the case. Unless he could present some solid evidence that Cella had been at the scene of the crime, Cella would go free.

The prosecutor had one last chance to win the case. He decided to take it.

A detective dusts for fingerprints on a stolen car.

"Your honor," he said, "I call Detective Sergeant Joseph A. Faurot to the stand."

Every eye in the courtroom was on the young detective as he came forward. Sergeant Faurot took the stand and calmly answered the prosecutor's questions in a strong, clear voice.

"Did you examine the scene of the crime, Sergeant Faurot?" asked the prosecutor.

"Yes," replied Sergeant Faurot.

"Did you discover anything important?"

"I found some marks on a window frame."

"What kind of marks?"

"The prints of several dirty fingers."

"And why are these prints important?"

"I have been studying a new method that allows me to identify a person by his or her fingerprints," replied Faurot. "In fact, over the last few years I have collected samples of the fingerprints of a number of criminals."

"Were you able to match the prints from the window frame to any of your samples?"

"Yes, I was," said Faurot, turning to the jury. "The fingerprints at the crime scene are those of the defendant, Caesar Cella!"

Noisy confusion broke out in the courtroom. No one had ever heard of these "fingerprints" before. The judge banged his gavel and shouted, "Order!" Finally the people settled back into their seats, eager to see what would happen next. Would the judge accept this new evidence? Would a few dirty marks on a window frame be enough to convict Caesar Cella? Or would he go free?

Everyone who has ever read a mystery story or watched a police show on TV has heard about fingerprints. But what exactly are they? Look closely at the tips of your fingers. You will see each finger is covered with tiny ridges. These ridges make a pattern that never changes. When you touch something, oils from your skin leave a print of this pattern on the surface you touch. The pattern is your fingerprint.

But why do your fingers have ridges in the first place? The answer is simple. The ridges help you grasp and hold onto things. They act like the stick-ons some people put on the bottom of the bathtub to keep their feet from slipping. The ridges on your fingers, and also on the palms of your hands, keep things from slipping out of your hands.

Scientists divide fingerprints into different categories according to the patterns made by the ridges. The three basic patterns are loops, whorls, and arches. The amazing thing is, no two fingerprints are exactly alike. Each person's fingerprints are different from everyone else's. This is why fingerprints can be used to identify people.

Most of the fingerprints we leave behind are invisible to the naked eye. You really cannot see your fingerprints unless you touch something with dirty hands. But this does not mean criminals must have dirty hands before the police can find their fingerprints. To find the invisible fingerprints left by criminals, police detectives "dust" the scene of a crime. What they actually do is spread a thin layer of fine powder on the surface they want to test. The dusting powder sticks to the skin oils left behind by the criminal's fingers. When the detective brushes away the loose powder, the fingerprints become visible.

The prints are then photographed and kept as evidence. The prints are also removed, or lifted, with clear tape and placed on a fingerprint card.

Dusting for fingerprints works best on smooth, hard surfaces like glass or metal. To find prints on other surfaces, such as paper and wood, detectives use chemicals that darken when they come into contact with the skin oils.

When a suspect is arrested, police take a complete set of her or his fingerprints. They roll the suspect's fingertips in ink and then press them onto a fingerprint card. This card is stored in police files. Later, when the police find fingerprints at a crime scene, they compare the new prints to the fingerprints they have on file. Today, many police departments store their fingerprint files on computers. This makes it possible for police departments to store millions of fingerprints and to share them with other departments across the nation.

Without fingerprints it would be very hard for the police to solve crimes. But it was not until the late 1800s that the police began to become interested in fingerprints. People had been

A police officer fingerprints an arrested suspect. In most U.S. cities, every person arrested is fingerprinted.

aware of the ridges on their fingertips, but they had not thought of using them to solve crimes.

In the 1870s, William Herschel, a British official in India, began experimenting with fingerprints as a hobby. He collected prints from a number of people and studied them. After a while he realized that no two people's fingerprints were exactly alike. Herschel soon became excited about the possibility of using fingerprints as a way of identifying people.

Over the next 35 years, individual police officers such as Sergeant Faurot began to take notice of Herschel's discovery. They used fingerprinting in their own investigations. But there was no widespread system for fingerprinting criminals in the United States. By 1911, one important question still waited to be answered. Would fingerprints be accepted as evidence in a criminal trial?

After the people in the courtroom returned to order, Caesar Cella's lawyer rose up from his chair and prepared to cross-examine Sergeant Faurot.

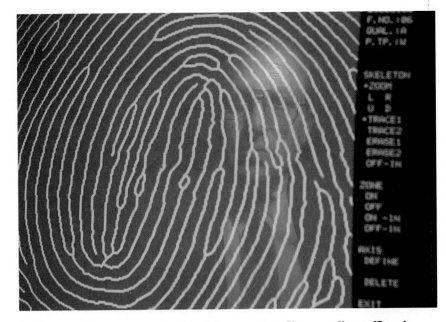

As he studies a computerized fingerprint file, a police officer's image is reflected on screen.

"Do you honestly expect us to trust these finger smudges over the sworn testimony of five people?" he asked. "Because either they are all liars or your little fingerprints are nothing more than pure bunk."

How was the jury to decide? This was the first time a court in the United States was being asked to convict a person solely on the evidence of fingerprints. No one wanted to risk sending an innocent person to jail. But Sergeant Faurot's testimony had been very convincing.

Finally the judge came up with an idea. He had Sergeant Faurot leave the courtroom. Then the judge asked fifteen people from the courtroom to press their right index fingers against the glass of the windows. One of the fifteen people was also asked to press the same finger against the glass on the top of the judge's desk.

The judge then sent for Faurot and asked him to identify which print on the windows matched the one on his glass desktop.

HOW TO PICK UP FINGERPRINTS

Fingerprints are great clues because no two prints are alike. So prints on file with the police department are easy to trace. Here's what you need to know in order to pick up prints left behind at the scene of a crime.

What you'll need:

- Talcum powder or ground chalk for picking up prints on dark surfaces.

- Dark powder for lifting prints from light surfaces. You can make your own by scraping the lead from a pencil using sandpaper or a nail file. Or use ground charcoal.

- An artist's paintbrush, with bristles about 1/2" wide.

- Transparent tape (at least 1" wide works best).

Faurot took out a large magnifying glass and went to work studying the prints. Within four minutes he identified the correct print. The jury stared at Faurot, their mouths hanging open in awe. Some people in the courtroom actually started to clap.

Faced with this proof of the power of fingerprints, Cella admitted everything. He said he had indeed gone to the show that night, and then to bed. But after his wife fell asleep, he sneaked out of the house and broke into the shop. He then returned home and to bed without even waking her.

This case was an historic event. For the first time, a United States court had accepted fingerprints as evidence in a criminal trial. In the years that followed, many other criminals found themselves in Caesar Cella's shoes. They were convicted on the evidence of their own fingertips.

What to do:

1. Make a clear fingerprint by pressing your thumb down firmly on a smooth, flat surface. Try a countertop or a drinking glass.

2. Pour a bit of fingerprint powder over the print. Using the paintbrush, dust the powder lightly over the print. Gently brush away the loose powder.

3. Place a piece of tape firmly over the powder print. Use your fingernail to press the tape down.

4. Peel off the tape and stick it down on a piece of paper. Use light paper for dark-powdered prints and dark paper for light-powdered prints.

Try lifting existing prints off other smooth, flat surfaces. Start a fingerprint file with the prints you lift.

Important Dates

1250

The universal symbol of detectives—the magnifying glass—is invented.

1814

The first scientific paper on detecting poisons is published by Mathieu Orfila of France.

1838

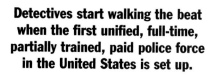

Detectives start walking the beat when the first unified, full-time, partially trained, paid police force in the United States is set up.

1950

The FBI begins its "Ten Most Wanted Fugitives" program. Posters are displayed across the country identifying wanted criminals.

1941

A new means of identification is introduced with the sound spectrograph, which produces voice prints of an individual's voice patterns.

1930

The Federal Bureau of Investigation (FBI) establishes a national fingerprint file.

1972

For the first time, the FBI employs female special agents to take on important and sometimes dangerous intelligence operations.

1980

Ray White of the United States discovers a controversial method of detecting differences in individuals' DNA.

1983

Police officers go high-tech when personal computers are introduced into patrol cars in the United States to record crime reports and access the FBI's National Crime Information Center.

76

in Crime Investigation

1850

Allan Pinkerton establishes the first private detective agency in the United States. The expression "private eye" begins in his office.

1887

Fictional detective Sherlock Holmes uses scientific methods of detection years before they are discovered by real detectives.

1892

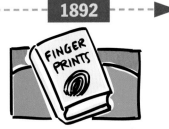

A scientific system of classifying fingerprints is developed by Francis Galton of England.

1920

Mystery writer Agatha Christie publishes her first novel, *The Mysterious Affair of Styles.*

1903

Proving that fingerprinting is more than a fad, New York City police officers begin routinely taking fingerprints of arrested persons.

1894

Writer Mark Twain popularizes the idea of fingerprinting in his short story, "The Tragedy of Pudd'n Head Wilson."

1987

For the first time in the United States, the DNA test is used as evidence to convict a person of a crime.

1993

Notebook-sized computers are developed for recording fingerprints and taking mug shots at a crime scene.

1994

Dramatic strides in laser technology make it possible to retrieve fingerprints from all kinds of sources.

Lilly Gallman

INKED PRINT

1
2
3
4
5
6
7
8
9
10

Forensic Chemist

This chemist *uses* science to solve crimes.

When investigators are called to the scene of the crime, the search for clues begins right away. But they can't analyze the evidence by themselves. They rely on the help of experts with the scientific knowledge to tell them what each clue means. That's where a forensic chemist like Lilly Gallman comes in. Gallman knows how to turn clues into solutions!

PROFILE

Name: Lilly Gallman

Home: Columbia, South Carolina

Occupation: forensic chemist (a scientist who helps solve crimes)

Education: college degree in biology; special studies in crime detection with the Federal Bureau of Investigation (FBI)

First investigative job: genetic researcher for the University of South Carolina

Favorite TV detective: Columbo

QUESTIONS

for Lilly Gallman

Find out **how** *forensic chemist* **Lilly Gallman helps** take a *bite* out of crime!

 How do you get involved with a case?

 When police are called to investigate a crime scene, they'll contact me. Sometimes I get called at four in the morning and don't get home until the next day.

Q **What's the first thing you do at a crime scene?**

A I examine the area carefully to see if the suspect left any physical evidence. If so, we can use that evidence to link the suspect with the crime.

 What kinds of things do you look for?

 Footprints, clothing fibers, strands of hair, fingerprints, things like that.

 What happens then?

A We take the clues back to the lab and analyze them. I send stray hairs and fibers to be analyzed under an electron microscope.

If the police arrest a suspect, I go to the police station. Sometimes I need to interview the suspect about the crime. Sometimes I take the suspect's shoes or clothing. I make plaster casts of the shoes to see if they match footprints left at the crime scene. I find out if fibers from the suspect's clothing match fibers at the crime scene.

Q Does your job end there?

 A No. After I'm done examining the clues, I've got to write up a report for the investigating officer on the case. The officer will meet with me to discuss the report, and later on I may be called on to testify in court.

Q Is your job really like what we see on TV?

A Not really. The so-called forensic people on TV often use methods that don't really work. Further, they usually pick up important clues in a matter of seconds. It rarely happens that way. It sometimes takes hours to find good clues at the scene of the crime.

 Q What was the best clue you ever found?

A We had a burglar who left his wallet at the scene of the crime. The wallet had his driver's license in it, so we got him immediately. We couldn't ask for a better clue than that!

TIPS Lilly Gallman's for Young Problem Solvers

1 Be a careful observer. Keep an eye out for the unusual.

2 Think logically. Be aware of causes and effects.

3 Be patient. Take the time to thoroughly think through problems and puzzles.

How to
Write a Mini-Mystery

Almost everyone loves to solve a mystery, at least when it's contained between the covers of a book. Mystery stories, long or short, allow armchair detectives to match wits with fiction's sharpest sleuths and sneakiest villains.

What is a mini-mystery? A mini-mystery is a mystery story that is just a few short paragraphs or pages long. Like every mystery, it includes a problem or question, clues, and a solution. Unlike most longer mysteries, a mini-mystery is often built around one main clue.

Here's the problem—how to prove that Tilford's scheme is a scam.

This seemingly ordinary statement contains the main clue.

Additional clues are given to wrap up the mystery.

The Case of the Buried Treasure

"From the gleam in your eye, I deduce you are about to get rich quick," said Dr. Haledjian.

"Clever of you, old chap," said Bertie Tilford, a young Englishman with a superiority complex toward work. "If I had a mere ten thousand I should realize a fortune! Have you ten?"

"What's the game now?" demanded Haledjian. "Pieces of eight among the corals? Doubloons from Kidd's chest?"

Bertie opened a sack and triumphantly produced a shining silver candlestick. "Sterling silver," he said. "See what's engraved on the bottom."

Haledjian upended the candlestick and read the name Lady North. "Wasn't that the ship that sank in 1956?"

"The Lady North sank, but not with all hands as is generally believed," replied Bertie. "Four men got away with a fortune in loot before the ship capsized in the storm.

"They hid their loot in a cave," continued Bertie. "But the storm started an avalanche and sealed off the entrance, burying three of the sailors inside. The fourth, a chap named Pembroot, escaped. Pembroot's been trying to raise ten thousand to buy the land on which the cave is located."

"You put up the money, the cave is opened, and the loot is divided two ways instead of four. Enchanting," said Haledjian. "Only how do you know Pembroot isn't a swindler?"

"Earlier tonight he took me to the cave," said Bertie. "This sack was half buried in the bushes, and I nearly sprained my ankle on it. I took one look and brought the candlestick here nonstop. You've got to agree it's the real thing, old chap."

"It is," admitted Haledjian. "And there's no doubt that Pembroot planted it by the cave for your benefit." How did Haledjian know?

An "expert" or detective, such as Haledjian, is a common character in mini-mysteries.

Here's the solution!

If the silver candlestick had been lying in a sack since 1956, it would have been tarnished, not "shining."

1 Brainstorm a Main Clue

In the mini-mystery you just read, the most important clue lies in the description of the candlestick. Before you begin to write your mini-mystery, you should come up with a similar clue.

TOOLS

- Paper and pencil
- Art supplies (optional)

Your clue should be a story detail that couldn't really have happened or couldn't really be true, for example, a bogus "cave-painting" that shows people hunting dinosaurs. The painting couldn't be authentic because dinosaurs became extinct before people existed.

2 Create Characters

Now that you've come up with a main clue, you can decide what sort of characters will be involved in your mystery. You'll probably want to create at least two characters. One, like Tilford, will stumble onto or uncover the mystery, and the other, like Haledjian, will solve it. Their identities will probably be related to the main clue. For example, if your clue is about a phony "rare" coin, your characters might be a coin collector or dealer and a quick-thinking expert in rare coins.

Tip Your mystery will be easier to write if you avoid creating too many characters. As your story progresses, write out any characters who are not important to the plot.

3 Outline Your Plot

It's time to incorporate your characters and your clue into a mystery story. Remember that your clue should lead to the solution to a question or problem. For example, perhaps the coin collector from Step 2 wants to buy a rare coin but suspects it's a fake. His or her problem is how to tell whether the coin is authentic. A main clue—some type of information about rare coins—will lead to the answer. Write a plot outline briefly describing the main events of your mini-mystery. In your outline, you should note the following:

• the mystery problem or question

• who encounters the problem/ question and how

• the main clue

• how the main clue is revealed or discovered

• any additional clues

• who solves the mystery

4 Write Your Mini-Mystery

By now, you should be ready to write a mini-mystery! Use your plot outline as a guide. Write up your mystery, filling in all the details that go with each event on the outline. When you're done with your first draft, check your work carefully. Make sure that your mystery "works." Does the solution really solve the mystery? Does the clue really lead to the solution? Make any necessary revisions or corrections. When your work is complete, swap mysteries with a classmate. Try to solve each other's!

If You Are Using a Computer ...

Draft your mini-mystery in the Newsletter format on your computer. Write an intriguing headline to draw your readers into the mystery.

THINK

How can asking the right questions help you become a better problem solver?

Lilly Gallman
Forensic Chemist ▶

CLUES

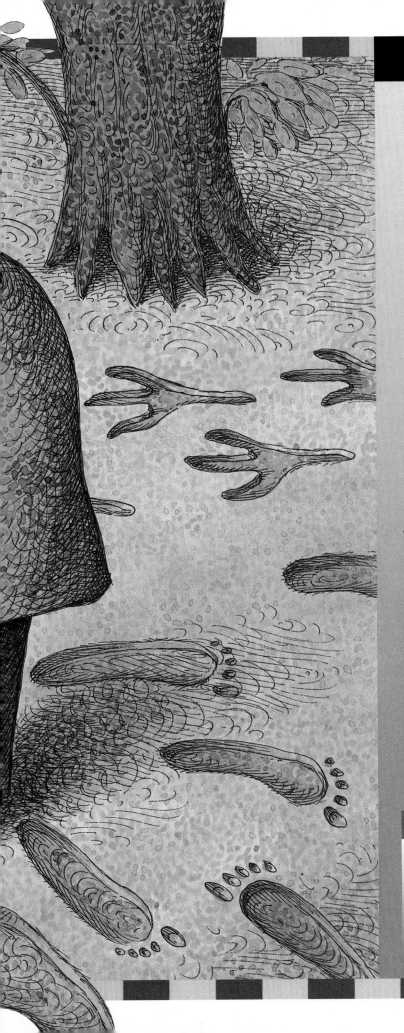

There are mysteries in the world
that still puzzle us.

Real-World Mysteries

Join archaeologist
Sara Bisel as she
uncovers the secrets
of an ancient city.

Read about
Boston's Gardner
Museum heist and
other unsolved
mysteries from
around the world.

PROJECT

Study a real-world mystery
and write an investigative
report about it.

MAYAN
PYRAMIDS
INVESTIGATIVE REPORT

87

FROM
THE
SECRETS
OF
VESUVIUS

By Sara C. Bisel

AWARD
WINNING

Book

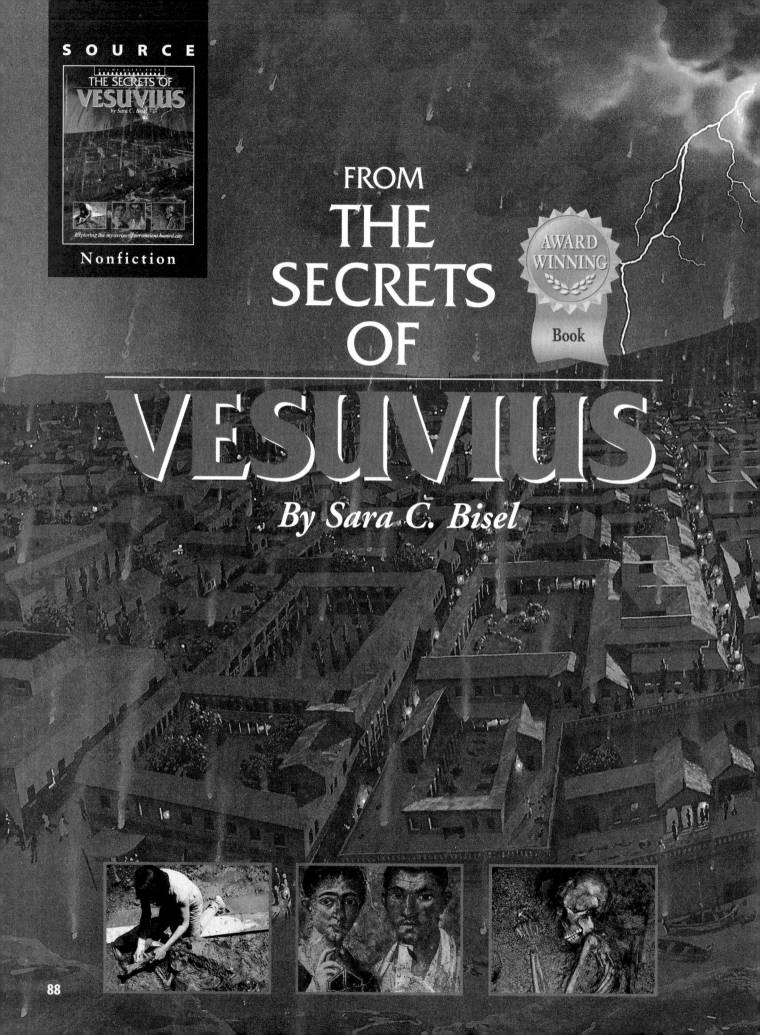

When Mount Vesuvius erupted almost 2,000 years ago, it poured volcanic ash and boiling mud down upon the Roman town of Herculaneum. By the time the fiery avalanche had cooled, thousands of townspeople and many of the buildings lay preserved beneath sixty-five feet of hardened lava.

For years, archaeologists have been excavating the ruins of Herculaneum in search of artifacts that would tell them more about ancient Roman civilization. Then in 1982 they made a crucial discovery—a group of skeletons was found on a beach at the foot of the town. They quickly called in Dr. Sara Bisel, "The Bone Lady." Dr. Bisel began to examine the skeletons for clues about the lives of the inhabitants of Herculaneum. In this excerpt from her book, her findings bring to life the story of that fateful day in A.D. 79, when Mount Vesuvius stopped history dead in its tracks.

The People
on the Beach

Herculaneum, June 1982

It was quiet on Herculaneum's ancient beach. Above my head, drying sheets and underwear fluttered from the apartment balconies that now overlook the ruins.

Today this beach is just a narrow dirt corridor that lies several feet below sea level. But thousands of years ago, the waves of the Mediterranean would have lapped where I now stood, and my ears would have been filled with the gentle sound of the surf, rather than the dull roar of Ercolano's midday traffic.

To one side of me stood the arched entryways of the boat chambers, most of them still plugged by volcanic rock, their secrets locked inside. Only one chamber had been opened so far, and its contents were now hidden behind a padlocked plywood door.

I eyed the wooden door longingly, wishing for a sudden gift of X-ray vision. Dr. Maggi, the keeper of the key, had been called away to a meeting with some government officials, and would not be back until sometime in the afternoon.

"Dottoressa!"

Ciro was calling me from farther down the old beach. He was waving me toward a roped-off area surrounding three ordinary-looking piles of dirt.

I have examined thousands of skeletons in my life, but seeing each one for the first time still fills me with a kind of awe. As I walked over to the mound that Ciro was pointing at, I knew I was about to meet my first Herculanean.

It didn't look like much at first—just a heap of dirt with bits of bone poking out. I knelt down and gently scraped earth off the skeleton, exposing it to the light for the first time in two thousand years. Although the skeleton was badly broken, I had a hunch that it might be female, but I was puzzled by the position of her bones. Her thigh was poking out grotesquely beside a section of skull. It almost looked as if the bones had been carelessly tossed there, they were so broken and tangled.

Then I realized that something dreadful had happened to this woman, and that she had met with a violent death of some kind. Her skull was shattered, her pelvis crushed, and her leg had been thrust up to her neck. Roof tiles were trapped beneath her.

I looked up. Above me was the open terrace where Herculaneans had held sacred ceremonies. Above that was the wall of the town itself, most of the surrounding balustrade now missing.

Had this woman fallen from the wall above? Had some huge force propelled her from the town, perhaps a piece of flying debris, or the blast from the volcano itself, so that she smashed face down onto the ground? What had she been doing on the wall in the first place? Calling down to the people on the beach for help?

Above: The beachfront, the ruins of Herculaneum and Vesuvius as they look today.

I picked up one of the bones and felt its cool smoothness in my hands. Because this was the first Herculanean I got to know, this skeleton was extra special to me. I named her Portia.

By measuring the bones, I could tell that Portia was about 5 feet 1 inch (155 centimeters) tall. She was about forty-eight when she died—an old woman by Roman standards—and had buck teeth.

Later, after a chemical analysis, we learned that Portia also had very high levels of lead in her bones. Lead is a poison, but in Roman times it was a common substance. It was used in makeup, medicines, paint pigment, pottery glazes, and to line drinking cups and plates.

On either side of Portia was a skeleton. One was another female. She lay on her side, almost looking as if she had died in her sleep. As I brushed dirt from her left hand, something shiny caught my eye as it glinted in the sunlight. It was a gold ring.

When we uncovered the rest of the hand, we found a second ring. And in a clump on her hip we found two intricate snakes' head bracelets made of pure gold, a pair of earrings that may have held pearls, and some coins (the cloth purse that had probably once held these valuables had long since rotted away).

We ended up calling her the Ring Lady. She was about forty-five when she died. She was not terribly good-looking; her jaw was large and protruding. There were no cavities in her teeth, but she did have gum disease, which left tiny pits in the bone along her gum line. If she had lived today, her dentist probably would have advised her to floss more often!

Right: I carefully place each bone in a plastic vegetable crate to be transported to my laboratory.

We called this skeleton the Ring Lady because of the two gold rings she wears on her left hand. We also found two bracelets, a pair of earrings and some coins by her side.

In fact, most of the Herculaneans I examined had very good teeth, with only about three cavities each. Today, many of us have about sixteen cavities each, in spite of all our fluoride treatments, regular dental checkups and constant nagging to floss and brush! But the Romans had no sugar in their diet. They used honey, but not much, because it was expensive. Instead, the Herculaneans ate a well-balanced diet, including much seafood, which is rich in fluoride. Not only that, but they had strong jaws from chewing and tearing food without using knives and forks. And they did clean their teeth, scrubbing them with the stringy end of a stick rather than using a brush and toothpaste.

On the other side of Portia we dug up the skeleton we called the Soldier. He was found lying face down, his hands outstretched, his sword still in his belt. We found carpenter's tools with him, which had perhaps been slung over his back. (Roman soldiers often worked on building projects when they were between wars.) He also had a money belt containing three gold coins. He was quite tall for a Roman, about 5 feet 8 inches (173 centimeters).

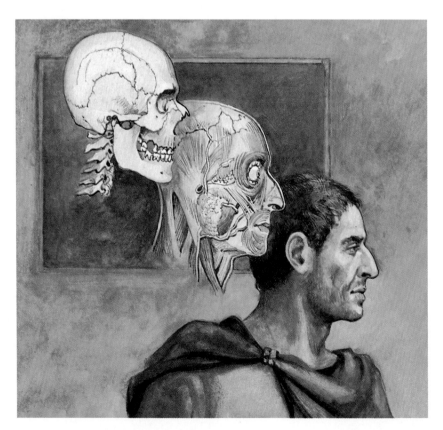

Right: When I examine a skull closely, I can usually tell what kind of features a person had. The soldier's skull, for example, shows that he had a large nose. By "clothing" the skull with muscles and nerves, we can show what the soldier might have looked like.

When I examined the man's skull, I could see that he was missing six teeth, including three at the front, and that he'd had a huge nose. And when I examined the bone of his left thigh, I could see a lump where a wound had penetrated the bone and caused a blood clot that eventually had hardened. Near the knee, where the muscle would have been attached, the bone was enlarged slightly. This indicated that he would have had well-developed thighs, possibly due to gripping the sides of a horse with the knees while riding (Romans didn't use saddles).

Had the soldier lost those front teeth in a fight, I wondered. Had he been wounded in the leg during the same fight or another one? His life must have been fairly rough and tumble.

While members of the excavation team poured buckets of water on the three skeletons to loosen the debris, I continued to scrape off the dirt and volcanic matter with a trowel. Later, in the laboratory, each bone and tooth would be washed with a soft brush. Then they would be left to dry before being dipped in an acrylic solution to preserve them. Finally, each bone would be measured, then measured again to prevent errors, and the figures would be carefully recorded.

By late afternoon my back and knees were stiff from crouching, and the back of my neck was tight with the beginning of a sunburn.

I stood up and stretched. There was still much to do before the three skeletons would be free of their volcanic straitjackets. I started to think about heading back to the hotel for a shower and bite to eat. But a flurry of activity down the beach caught my eye, and suddenly I no longer felt tired.

To my right, Dr. Maggi stood outside the locked wooden door I had seen earlier. He was unbolting the padlock. When he saw me, he waved. I put down my trowel, wiped my hands on my jeans and hurried over. Inside, I knew, was the only group of Roman skeletons that had ever been found—the twelve people who had huddled in the shelter and died together when the volcanic avalanches poured down the mountainside into the sea.

I could hear an odd echo from inside the chamber as Dr. Maggi clicked the padlock open. Behind me, a number of the crew members had gathered. We were all very quiet.

The plywood door seemed flimsy as Dr. Maggi pulled it open. From inside the chamber came the dank smell of damp earth.

A shiver crept up my neck. We were opening a 2,000-year-old grave. What would we find?

As I entered the cave-like boat chamber, I could barely see, even though the sun flooded through the door. Someone handed me a flashlight, but its light cast greenish shadows, making it feel even more spooky.

The light played over the back of the shelter, no bigger than a single garage and still crusted over with volcanic rock. I saw an oddly shaped, lumpy mound halfway back. I took several steps into the chamber and pointed the light at the mound.

The narrow beam found a skull, the pale face a grimace of death. As my eyes grew accustomed to the dim light, I soon realized there were bones and skulls everywhere. They were all tangled together—clinging to each other for comfort in their final moments—and it was hard to distinguish one from another. But I knew that twelve skeletons had been found in all—three men, four women and five children. One child had an iron house key near him. Did he think he would be going back home?

I took another step into the cave. At my feet was a skeleton that was almost entirely uncovered. From the pelvis I could see it was a female, a girl, lying face down. Beneath her, we could just see the top of another small skull.

It was a baby.

I knelt down and gently touched the tiny skull. My throat felt tight as I thought about this girl, this baby,

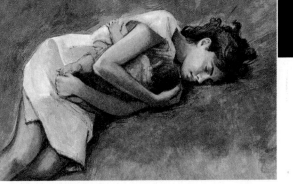

One of our most moving finds was the skeleton of a young slave girl cradling the tiny skull of a baby (*above*). With these two skeletons, the tragedy of that terrible day in A.D. 79 became very real to us.

and what it must have been like for them in this dark cave in the moments before they died.

"*Una madre col suo bambino,*" whispered Ciro behind me.

"I don't think they're a mother and baby," I said. I could see from the pelvis that the girl was not old enough to have had children. I pointed to my own stomach and outlined a beachball tummy with my arms while I shook my head.

"This girl has never given birth."

"*Allora, è la sorella?*"

I frowned, pulled my Italian-English dictionary out of the back pocket of my jeans and flipped through it. I realized Ciro thought these two skeletons belonged to a baby and its older sister.

"We'll see," I murmured. I knew it was important not to jump to conclusions.

You have to question everything about bones, especially ones that have been lying around for two thousand years. I've known cases where people thought bone damage was caused by joint disease, when it was in fact caused by rats gnawing at the dead body.

I struggled to free a bronze cupid pin and two little bells from the baby's bones. Whoever the child was, it had been rich enough to wear expensive ornaments. But I knew it would take many more hours of careful study before we knew the real story behind these two skeletons.

Later, in the laboratory, I gained enough information to put together a more likely background for the skeleton of the young girl.

Unlike the baby, she had not come from a wealthy family. She had been about fourteen, and from the shape of her skull I knew she had probably been pretty. When I examined her teeth I could tell that she had been starved or quite ill for a

WHAT BONES TELL US

The human skeleton contains about two hundred bones. Bones are rigid because they contain calcium — the same substance that is in eggshells and teeth. While you are alive, your bones are alive, too. Blood runs through them, they have their own nerves, and they grow and change shape and absorb chemicals, just like the rest of your body.

Once a body is dead, after the clothes and flesh have rotted away, the hard skeleton still holds many clues as to what the person was like when he or she was alive.

By "reading" and analyzing a skeleton, scientists can discover the person's sex, race and height. We can see approximately how old a person was at death, and approximately how many children a woman had. By looking at the way people's bones and teeth are formed, we can also tell whether they had certain diseases, or whether they had been starved or sick as children. If we grind up a small piece of bone and put it in a chemical solution, we can analyze the solution in a laboratory and find out what minerals have been absorbed by the bone, which can tell us what kind of food the person ate.

Muscles are attached to bones. When muscles are used frequently, they become bigger and pull on the places where they are attached. The bones will change time when she was a baby. She had also had two teeth removed about one or two weeks before she died, probably giving her a fair bit of pain. And her life had been very hard. She had done a lot of running up and down stairs or hills, as well as having to lift objects too heavy for her delicate frame.

This girl could not have been the child of a wealthy family, like the baby. She had probably been a slave who died trying to protect the baby of the family she worked for.

shape to create more surface for the muscles to attach to. By examining the shape and weight of certain bones, we can see which muscles were used, and what kind of work or exercise a person might have done.

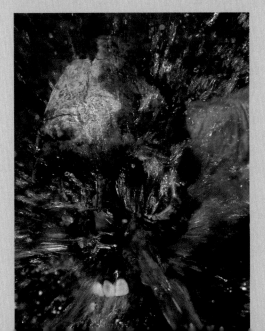

And there were many others. Near the slave girl lay the skeleton of a seven-year-old girl whose bones also showed that she had done work far too heavy for a child so young.

We found a sixteen-year-old fisherman, his upper body well developed from rowing boats, his teeth worn from holding cord while he repaired his fishing nets.

Particularly heartbreaking were the two pregnant women I examined, for we were also able to recover their tiny unborn babies, their bones as fragile as eggshells. One woman had been only about sixteen years old.

Though it is fascinating to reconstruct the life of a single person by examining his or her bones, for anthropologists and historians the most useful information comes from examining all of the skeletons of one population. This is one reason why Herculaneum is so important.

During the next few months we opened two more boat chambers. In one we discovered forty tangled human skeletons and one of a horse; in another we found twenty-six skeletons creepily lined up like a row of dominoes, as if heading in single file for the back of the chamber.

The skeletons represented a cross-section of the population of a whole town—old people, children and babies, slaves, rich and poor, men and women, the sick and the healthy. By examining all these skeletons, we can get some ideas about how the townspeople lived and what they were like physically.

We found out, for example, that the average Herculanean man was 5 feet 5 inches (165 centimeters) tall, the average woman about 5 feet 1 inch (155 centimeters). In general, they were well nourished. And we have examined enough people to know that although the rich people had easy lives, the slaves often worked so hard that they were in pain much of the time.

Studying these skeletons closely can also help medical researchers and doctors. In ancient times, many diseases could not be cured by surgery or drugs. Instead, people kept getting sicker, until they eventually died. By examining the bones of these people, we can learn a great deal about how certain diseases progress.

By the end of my stay in Herculaneum, I had examined 139 skeletons. Their bones were sorted into yellow plastic vegetable crates that lined the shelves in my laboratory. And each box of bones has a different story to tell.

Even though I can't tell the good guys from the bad, and I can't tell you whether they were happy or not, I know a great deal about these people. I can see each person plainly. I even imagine them dressed as they might have been, lounging on their terraces or in the baths if they were wealthy, toiling in a mine or in a galley if they were the most unfortunate slaves.

Most of all, I feel that these people have become my friends, and that I have been very lucky to have had a part in bringing their stories to the rest of the world.

Left: The Romans usually cremated the dead and placed their ashes in urns like this one.

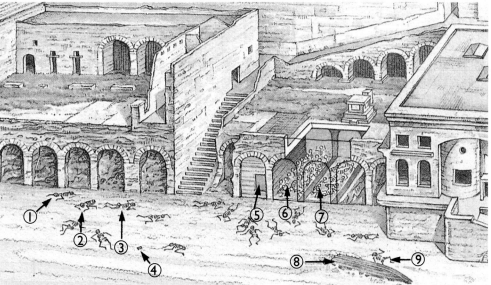

Who Were the People On the Beach?

The illustration *(above)* shows how the ancient seawall looks today. Altogether, we excavated over one hundred skeletons from the beach and boat chambers.

1. The Ring Lady
2. Portia
3. The Soldier
4. Coin box
5. Chamber with 26 skeletons inside
6. Chamber with 40 skeletons inside, including one of a horse
7. Petronia's chamber, with 12 skeletons inside
8. The boat
9. A slave, perhaps a fisherman

Above: Sometimes it can take as long as four days to glue a skull back together.

Left: Among the ruins archaeologists found these unusual glass beads with tiny faces on them.

On the rainy night of March 18, 1990, the Isabella Stewart Gardner Museum in Boston was robbed of priceless art treasures. Many different experts have worked for countless hours trying to solve the crime. However, the Gardner Museum heist has baffled even the best solution specialists.

From **The**

$200m Gardner Museum art theft

2 men posing as police tie up night guards

Boston's Gardner Museum was the site of an art theft last night.

By Andy Dabilis and John Ellemont

In what was described as the biggest art theft since the 1911 robbery of the *Mona Lisa,* two men posing as police officers gained entry to the Isabella Stewart Gardner Museum early yesterday, restrained two security guards and left with an estimated $200 million worth of art, police said.

The works stolen included paintings by Jan Vermeer, Rembrandt and Edgar Degas, museum officials said.

In a daring, middle-of-the-night robbery, police said, the two men knocked on a side door of the world-famous Gardner in Boston's Fenway

Boston Globe

MONDAY, MARCH 19, 1990

section at about 1:15 A.M. and told the security guards there was a disturbance in the area, and were allowed to enter.

Police and FBI officials said the men then overcame the guards, tied them with tape and spent about two hours in the museum, stealing 12 art objects.

Acting curator Karen Haas said the $200 million estimate is conservative, and the worth of the stolen works may be "hundreds of millions of dollars." She said they are considered priceless because they have not been on the market for nearly a century, and their value to private collectors is unknown.

Measured by the potential value of the art, the theft was considered the biggest ever in the United States, and perhaps the greatest ever verified for any crime, according to law enforcement officials, art experts and records kept on crime and art theft.

Two Guards Discovered

Boston police were called to the scene shortly after a maintenance worker discovered the two guards at

Vermeer's *The Concert* was the most valuable painting taken.

about 7 A.M. Police contacted the FBI, which has art experts on its staff.

The two guards were questioned extensively. Law enforcement sources said investigators are trying to learn whether the robbery was staged in order to ransom back the heavily insured objects, or to sell them to a private collector, since they are considered unmarketable otherwise.

FBI agent Fred Cavanagh said, "This is one of those thefts where people actually spent some time researching and took specific things. The job was a professional job."

MARCH 19, 1990

Secret collector's passion or ransom seen as motive

By Peter S. Canellos
GLOBE STAFF

The art treasures seized from the Isabella Stewart Gardner Museum yesterday were probably contracted for in advance by a collector outside the country, private investigators and art experts theorized yesterday.

Stolen pieces of the importance of those in yesterday's robbery could have been taken only for one of two purposes, they said: for sale to a collector who had already agreed to buy them or for possible ransom.

But the thieves appeared to have set their sights on specific works, having left behind many of equal or greater value. This indicates that one particular buyer's tastes may have been indulged, the sources added.

"There probably was a contract for these paintings," said Charles Moore, a Brockton detective who has recovered about $20 million worth of art through 10 highly publicized cases. "It could just be a collector who wanted them."

Moore said he thinks the works are already headed for South America or Japan. "That's where the money is," Moore said.

Hidden Collections Rumored

For years, such missing masterpieces have been rumored to be part of the hidden collections of foreign millionaires.

Walter Kaiser, director of Itatti, the Harvard University art study center in Florence, Italy, said in an interview yesterday that "Everyone hears stories about South American millionaires who sit in their basements and look at paintings no one else can be allowed to see. But you never know whether they're true."

Moore, for one, said he believes eccentric collectors of stolen art do exist. But he said that such collectors would be very difficult to contact, unless one of them indicated his or her interest in advance. If the thieves have not already cut a deal, he added, their best chance to make money would be to sell them back to the Gardner Museum or its insurance company.

THIEVES MAY FIND THE BOOTY TOO HOT TO HANDLE

By Renee Graham
GLOBE STAFF

There is no Dr. No.

So say art experts concerning common theories of sinister rich collectors who, like the James Bond supervillain, arrange thefts of priceless works or are willing to purchase such objects. Unless the thieves who plundered the Isabella Stewart Gardner Museum had a pre-arranged buyer, these priceless works of art stolen Sunday are virtually worthless.

"They're unsalable. There's no place for them in the legitimate market," said Constance Lowenthal, executive director of the International Foundation for Art Research, a New York organization that documents art thefts. "They're too hot to handle.

"And as far as a collector who orders a theft, we don't have a single documented case of a Dr. No," she said. "It's all speculation."

Dr. No

Who Is Dr. No?

Doctor No was a villain in a novel (and movie) by Ian Fleming, featuring special agent James Bond. In the story, Dr. No ordered the theft of a famous paint-ing for his secret art collection.

As they investigated the case, the Boston Globe decided to interview a different kind of expert — a professional art thief. In this article, "Lou" tells his theory about how the theft was masterminded.

Veteran Thief Says Robbery of Museum Would Be Easy

By Larry Tye
GLOBE STAFF

Lou knew full well how grand the Gardner Museum's collection was and how easy it would be to take—but he says he and other art-loving thieves were too enamored of the museum to rob it.

"The Gardner was my favorite place. Without a doubt it's the most beautiful museum of art in the world," the 52-year-old bank robber, burglar and art thief extraordinaire explained last week at a prison in Massachusetts where he is completing a nine-year sentence.

"It absolutely would have been easy to rob, but I went there as a visitor."

Who pulled the $200 million heist? "Either professional thieves who wanted a ransom or the IRA or some other terrorist group," said Lou, who asked that his full name and address be withheld because he fears that the FBI will try to use him as an intermediary with the Gardner thieves or that the gangsters will suspect that he is working with the police.

Where are the Vermeer, Rembrandt, and other stolen paintings? "Sitting in someone's temperature-controlled refrigerator. I bet they haven't even left this state. They're too well-known to move them anywhere," said Lou, who has the credentials to offer an educated guess.

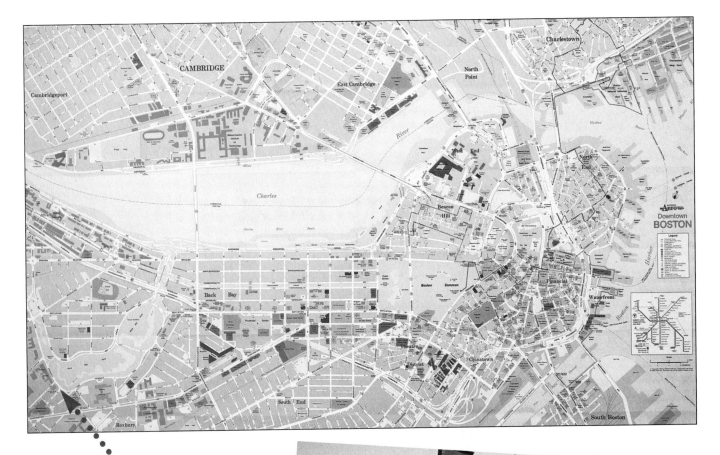

The Gardner Museum is tucked away behind a fence on a small hill. It is about two miles outside of downtown Boston and is surrounded by hospitals, colleges, and museums.

Weeks passed, and the police and the FBI still weren't able to name the person or persons behind the crime. But they were able to put together a picture of exactly what happened the night the paintings were stolen. In this article, you'll see how one expert puts together an investigative report showing how the thieves pulled off the art heist of the century.

Retracing the steps of robbery's twisted trail

By Elizabeth Neuffer
GLOBE STAFF

Rain beat down on the Isabella Stewart Gardner Museum in the early morning of March 18.

Inside the palazzo-style museum, a young security guard sat in a cramped office. His eyes periodically scanned four television security monitors. A clock's hands crawled past 1 A.M.

It was a typical Sunday morning shift until the museum's doorbell rang. Two men in police uniforms said they had been called to investigate a disturbance. The guard, perplexed, let them in.

"You look familiar," one of the men reportedly told the dumbfounded guard. "Let me see your ID; I think I have a warrant for you."

The guard stepped forward, out from behind a counter and away from security alarms. He summoned his partner. Within minutes, it was done:

The guards were handcuffed, bound and gagged—not by two police officers, but by two thieves who had fooled them. The theft of an estimated $200 million in art—one of the largest heists in history—was under way.

What precisely happened that morning in carrying out the robbery is known only to the two thieves. But two months after the break-in, interviews with Boston police, the FBI, museum officials, former museum guards and security experts form a partial picture of the theft that devastated the eclectic museum in the Fenway and shocked the art world.

On the day before the robbery, 500 visitors admired the paintings scattered throughout three floors of the museum. But by midnight, two security guards had the museum entirely to themselves.

The two thieves, having donned their police uniforms, had buzzed and demanded entry. The ruse of the arrest warrant had worked perfectly; both guards were taken by surprise.

The thieves shoved both guards up against a wall. Both were quickly handcuffed. They were led to the museum's dark basement, where they would spend six of the longest hours of their lives.

There, near a boiler and a work-bench, each guard was tied to a different utility pipe. Duct tape encircled their heads, vertically and horizontally. The thieves threatened to kill them.

One thief was in his late 30s, about 5 feet 9 inches, slim, with gold wire glasses and possibly a mustache; the other was in his early 30s, 6 feet tall, and heavier with chubby cheeks.

The thieves set to work in the darkened galleries. They appeared to know what they wanted; they bypassed artworks that were more valuable than the items they stole. In two hours, they stole 11 paintings and drawings, one vase and a finial from a flag.

Their route remains unclear. But security experts and authorities suspect that their first stop after the

The Men Who Broke In

Police artists drew sketches of the men who broke into the museum based on information from the museum guards. The men were sketched with and without mustaches, to show how they might change their appearances.

Suspect #1

Suspect #2

Suspect #1 with mustache

Suspect #2 with mustache

basement was to return to the guard watch desk.

Noticing that a camera was video-taping them, they yanked the camera around to face the wall. Tracing its wires to a nearby room, they destroyed the system's video cassette.

The thieves also tried to dismantle part of the museum's alarm system, which could track their footsteps through the building. Part of the system consisted of detectors in each gallery, which recorded movements and relayed the information to a central computer.

They turned off the computer printer, thinking that action would destroy any record of their presence. But they erred by leaving computer data that has shown details about their movements to investigators.

Even so, the alarm was worthless that morning without guards to notify the police. The Gardner Museum, like many museums, had no external alarms. With the guards trussed in the basement, the thieves were free to do their work.

The duo's first stop apparently was the second-floor Dutch Room, where six paintings were stolen.

Quickly, they set to work. One or both of the thieves wrested Rembrandt's only seascape, *The Storm on the Sea of Galilee* from the wall, carelessly dropping the frame on the floor. To steal *The Concert*, a 17th-century painting by Vermeer, and Govaert Plinck's *Landscape with an Obelisk*, they smashed the glass covering the canvases.

Authorities suspect that one of the thieves headed for the Short Gallery, also on the second floor, passing through two other galleries—one, the Early Italian Room, filled with Renaissance paintings and antique furniture, the other, the Raphael Room.

In the Short Gallery, one of the thieves violently ripped two framed sets of prints off the wooden partitions that displayed them, authorities believe. Soon, he held Degas sketches in his hand.

The Blue Room, on the ground floor near the museum's public entrance, may have been the thieves' last stop. There, they yanked a Manet oil, *Chez Tortoni,* from the security bolts that fastened it to the wall.

Then, as easily as they had entered the Gardner, the thieves exited it. Perhaps a getaway car was waiting.

It was probably after 3 A.M.

The Gardner Museum's Dutch Room.

110

What was taken, from where

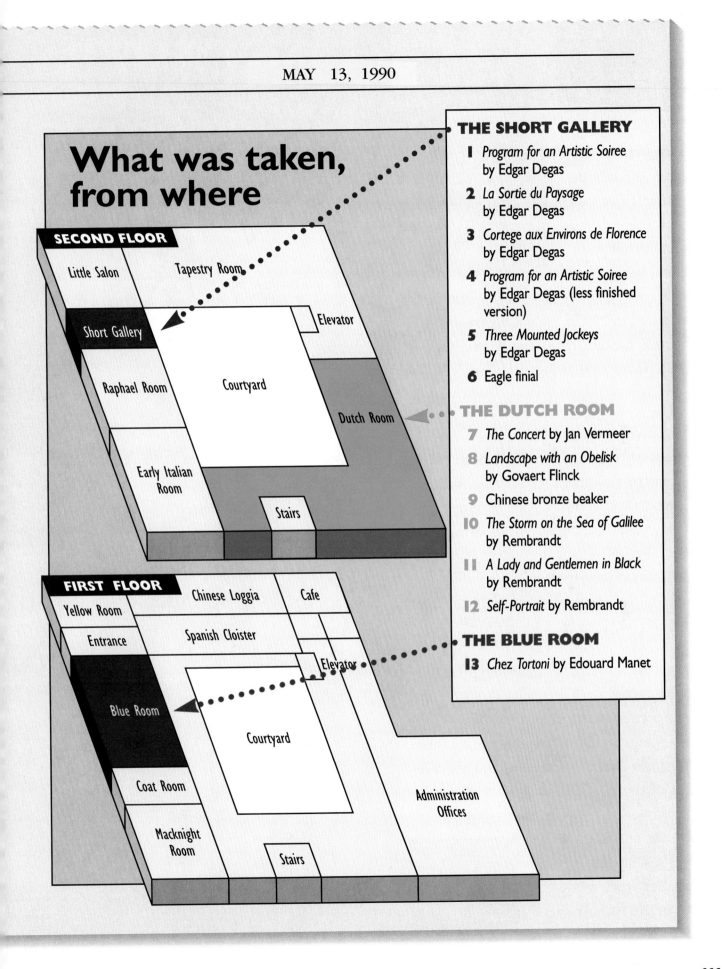

SECOND FLOOR

Little Salon
Tapestry Room
Short Gallery
Elevator
Raphael Room
Courtyard
Dutch Room
Early Italian Room
Stairs

FIRST FLOOR

Yellow Room
Chinese Loggia
Cafe
Entrance
Spanish Cloister
Elevator
Blue Room
Courtyard
Coat Room
Administration Offices
Macknight Room
Stairs

THE SHORT GALLERY

1 *Program for an Artistic Soiree* by Edgar Degas

2 *La Sortie du Paysage* by Edgar Degas

3 *Cortege aux Environs de Florence* by Edgar Degas

4 *Program for an Artistic Soiree* by Edgar Degas (less finished version)

5 *Three Mounted Jockeys* by Edgar Degas

6 Eagle finial

THE DUTCH ROOM

7 *The Concert* by Jan Vermeer

8 *Landscape with an Obelisk* by Govaert Flinck

9 Chinese bronze beaker

10 *The Storm on the Sea of Galilee* by Rembrandt

11 *A Lady and Gentlemen in Black* by Rembrandt

12 *Self-Portrait* by Rembrandt

THE BLUE ROOM

13 *Chez Tortoni* by Edouard Manet

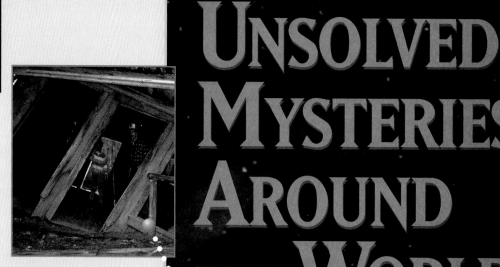

UNSOLVED MYSTERIES AROUND THE WORLD

The Oregon Vortex

Where in the world can you find a weird energy force? Try the Oregon Vortex and you'll find out. Objects in the Vortex seem to defy gravity. Before the eruption of Mt. St. Helens weakened the Vortex, brooms could stand erect for up to 36 hours—no strings attached.

The Disappearance of the Chaco Anasazi

Hundreds of years ago, Chaco Canyon was home to a people called the Anasazi. The Anasazi had complex road systems, five-story buildings, and advanced farming systems. But some time in the 13th century, they abandoned their homes rapidly, and no trace of them was ever found.

Easter Island

Imagine a strange island inhabited by giants—giants made of volcanic rock. Lined up along the shore of Easter Island are 300 statues of the bust of a man with long ears and a red headdress. The statues weigh up to 30 tons and average 12 feet high. Why and how the statues were made is one of the world's biggest mysteries.

On this map, you'll find some of the greatest unsolved mysteries from around the world. Are you familiar with any of them?

The Bermuda Triangle

Disappearing planes, vanishing ships—some people say the area of water known as the Bermuda Triangle is a dangerous trap for travelers. Over the years, many strange disappearances have been reported in the triangle. Is it true? Would you travel to the triangle to see for yourself?

The Last Flight of Amelia Earhart

One minute, she was making a historic plane flight around the world; the next minute, she was gone. The world was shocked when pilot Amelia Earhart vanished on May 20, 1937, somewhere over the Pacific. The secret of her disappearance may be lost beneath the sea forever.

The Ancient Mapmakers of Antarctica

For thousands of years, the coast of Antarctica has been buried under a hundred feet of ice. Complex equipment is needed to trace its coastline. But in 1929, Turkish officer Piri Réis found an old world map dated 1513 that included the coast of Antarctica! What ancient voyagers were able to travel to Antarctica and how did they map it? The answer may lie buried on the continent's icy shores.

How to
Prepare an Investigative Report

Use your *problem-solving* skills to *investigate* a real-life mystery!

Be a detective and investigate a real-life mystery that interests you. Perhaps you're curious about who built Stonehenge or why whales sometimes strand themselves on the beach. Whatever mystery you choose, you will research and analyze real-life clues and form a hypothesis about the solution to your mystery. Finally, you will gather your information into an investigative report.

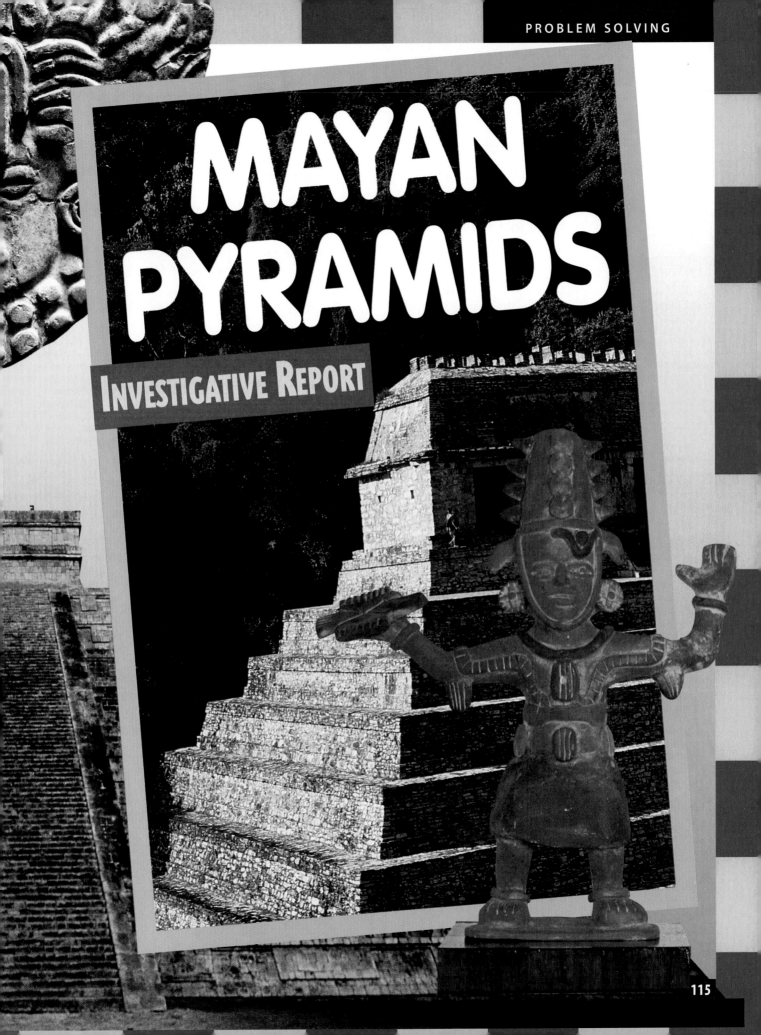

MAYAN PYRAMIDS

INVESTIGATIVE REPORT

1 Choose a Mystery

Mysteries have always existed and they continue to happen everyday. Why did the dinosaurs disappear? What became of the lost colony of Roanoke? Think of some other real-life mysteries of history and science. If you're having trouble coming up with ideas, you might return to "Unsolved Mysteries," do a little library research, or even check out a video about real-life mysteries. Once you've generated a list of possibilities, go over it and weed out those mysteries that may be impossible to research thoroughly. From the remaining list, select the mystery that intrigues you the most!

TOOLS

- Pencil and paper
- Folder
- Research materials

2 | Investigate the Mystery

Search for newspaper and magazine articles and nonfiction books that discuss your chosen mystery. Other possible sources of information include videos, TV programs, and people who are familiar with the subject. Find out what clues have already turned up in the search for a solution.

Make note of the hypotheses proposed by previous investigators. As you check out each source, take notes on the information you find, and file your notes in a folder. File, also, any pictures, charts, diagrams, or other visual aids that you might want to include in your report.

How Am I Doing?

Before you begin to analyze your research, take a minute to ask yourself these questions:

• Did I take clear notes on the mystery?

• Do my notes cover all possible angles?

• Did I use several sources of information so that my report will be as complete as possible?

Tip Keep a separate folder of notes about each hypothesis you study. That way, you'll be able to compare hypotheses easily.

Every investigative report includes a hypothesis, or guess, about what happened. A hypothesis is not a random guess, however, but one based on evidence. Look through your notes, and separate facts (those items which are positively known to be true) from opinions, or hypotheses.

List all the facts on the left side of a piece of paper and all the hypotheses on the right.

Look carefully at your lists. What do they tell you? By looking at the facts, can you eliminate any hypotheses? Which ones still seem possible?

Mayan stone carvings located in Rio Lacantun, Mexico, illuminated at night

4 Form Your Hypothesis

Review all the known facts about your mystery. Look once again at the hypotheses you have discarded and those that remain. Use your best judgment to come up with your own hypothesis. Check it against the facts. Is there reason to believe that your hypothesis could not possibly be correct? If so, revise it and check it against the facts once more.

5 Write Your Investigative Report

Introduce your report by describing your mystery. Next, list all the facts you've uncovered. Then, explain the different theories about solutions to the mystery, and why you did or did not discount them. If possible, enhance your report with some direct quotes, as well as with a variety of visual aids. Conclude by stating your hypothesis and explaining why you think it's the real solution! Finally, present your report to your classmates. Did other students investigate your mystery? Compare your report to theirs.

If You Are Using a Computer ...

Use the Report format on your computer to write your investigative report. Title it with a headline that will grab your readers' attention.

CONGRATULATIONS
You've become the detective in a real-world mystery! Keep your problem-solving skills sharp. You're sure to use them throughout your life.

Lilly Gallman
Forensic Chemist ▶

Glossary

ab·duct (ab dukt´) *verb*
To carry off by force; to kidnap.

a·gent (ā´jənt) *noun*
A person or business that acts as a representative of another person, business, or government agency.

am·bush
(am´boŏsh) *verb*
To attack from a hiding place.

an·thro·pol·o·gists
(an´thrə pol´ə jists) *noun*
Scientists who study the origins, development, communities, and customs of humans.
▲ **anthropologist**

Word History

The word **anthropologist** comes from the Greek words *anthropos*, meaning "human," and *logy*, meaning "the study of." An anthropologist is one who studies humans.

archaeologists

ar·chae·ol·o·gists
(är´kē ol´ə jists) *noun*
Scientists who study ancient times and ancient peoples. Archaeologists search for and examine the things left behind by ancient peoples in order to learn about them.
▲ **archaeologist**

back·ground
(bak´ground) *noun*
A person's origin, education, and experience. You need the right *background* to qualify for the job.

bi·zarre
(bi zär´) *adjective*
Very odd, strange; hard to believe.

blood·hound
(blud′hound′) *noun*
A large dog known for its
keen sense of smell.

boo·ty (boo͞′tē) *noun*
Loot; a group of things
that have been stolen or
taken by force.

ca·per
(kā′pər) *noun*
A criminal act or plan,
especially a robbery.

car·go
(kär′gō) *noun*
The load of goods carried
by a ship, airplane, or truck.

bloodhound

clues (kloo͞z) *noun*
Things that help to solve
mysteries. The problem
will be extremely difficult
to solve with so few *clues*.
▲ **clue**

com·mit·ted
(kə mit′əd) *verb*
Did something bad or
wrong. ▲ **commit**

con·vict (kən vikt′) *verb*
To prove someone guilty of
committing a crime.

de·fend·ant
(di fen′dənt) *noun*
A person who is charged
with a crime.

ev·i·dence
(ev′i dəns) *noun*
Something that provides
possible proof. A
fingerprint at the scene of
the crime is *evidence* of
who was there.

ex·ca·vat·ing
(eks′kə vāt′ing) *verb*
Uncovering by digging.
We will be rich as soon as
we finish *excavating* the
buried treasure.
▲ **excavate**

cargo

a	add	o͞o	took	ə =
ā	ace	o͞o	pool	a in *above*
â	care	u	up	e in *sicken*
ä	palm	û	burn	i in *possible*
e	end	yo͞o	fuse	o in *melon*
ē	equal	oi	oil	u in *circus*
i	it	ou	pout	
ī	ice	ng	ring	
o	odd	th	thin	
ō	open	th	this	
ô	order	zh	vision	

Glossary

fas·ci·nat·ed
(fas′ə nā′təd) *verb*
Aroused and held the
interest of. ▲ **fascinate**

gav·el (gav′əl) *noun*
A small wooden hammer
used by judges to call for
attention or quiet.

gavel

haul (hôl) *noun*
A load of goods to be
carried or transported.

hi·jack·ing
(hī′jak′ing) *verb*
Seizing by threat or force,
often for ransom, and
taken to a place that is not
the original destination.
▲ **hijack**

il·le·gal
(i lē′gəl) *adjective*
Against the law. Stealing is
illegal.

in·spired
(in spī′rd) *verb*
Caused or influenced
someone to do something.
▲ **inspire**

in·ter·cept
(in′tər sept′) *verb*
To stop or cut off
en route.

in·ves·ti·ga·tor
(in ves′ti gāt′ər) *noun*
Someone who looks into a
crime or other unusual
situation in order to learn
what really happened. The
investigator studied all of
the evidence to figure out
who was guilty.
▲ **investigate**

plun·dered
(plun′dərd) *verb*
Robbed by force, especially
during wartime.
▲ **plunder**

pros·e·cu·tor
(pros′i kyōō′tər) *noun*
A person, usually a lawyer,
who represents the state in
a courtroom proceeding
against someone who is
accused of a crime.

Fact File

A person accused of a serious
crime in the United States
has the right to a trial by a
jury, a group of 12 citizens.
The prosecutor's job is to
convince the jury that the
accused person is guilty. The
defense lawyer's job is to
convince the jury that the
accused person is innocent.
Witnesses tell what they
know about the crime. The
jury listens to the whole
case and then makes a
decision about it.

ran·som
(ran′səm) *noun*
The price for setting a
kidnapped person free.

re·mark·a·ble
(ri mär′kə bəl) *adjective*
Noteworthy; very unusual.

screech owl
(skrēch′oul′) *noun*
An owl that makes a very loud, shrill sound.

smug•glers
(smug′lərs) *noun*
People who bring illegal goods into or out of a country. ▲ **smuggler**

spec•u•la•tion
(spek′yə lā′shən) *noun*
A guess or theory.

sus•pi•cious
(sə spish′əs) *adjective*
That which causes one to suspect guilt or wrongdoing. When solving a crime, look out for *suspicious* activity.

tes•ti•fy (tes′tə fī′) *verb*
To give evidence under oath before a court.

screech owl

Fact File

The oath that witnesses must take before they **testify** in a court of law in the United States is as follows:

"I swear to tell the truth, the whole truth, and nothing but the truth."

theft (theft) *noun*
The act of stealing; robbery.

trow•el (trou′əl) *noun*
A tool with a pointed tip that is used for digging.

trowel

war•rant
(wôr′ənt) *noun*
An official paper that gives officers of the law the right to make an arrest, search property, or perform other acts needed to dispense justice.

a	add	o͝o	took	ə =
ā	ace	o͞o	pool	a in *above*
â	care	u	up	e in *sicken*
ä	palm	û	burn	i in *possible*
e	end	yo͞o	fuse	o in *melon*
ē	equal	oi	oil	u in *circus*
i	it	ou	pout	
ī	ice	ng	ring	
o	odd	th	thin	
ō	open	ŧh	this	
ô	order	zh	vision	

Authors & Illustrators

Sara C. Bisel *pages 88–101*

This author is known throughout the scientific community as one of the world's leading experts on ancient bones. She has worked on archaeological sites in Greece, Turkey, and Israel. When the exciting new finds were discovered at Herculaneum, Dr. Sara C. Bisel was on the scene. Her work has been featured in magazines such as *Discover* and *National Geographic*.

Barbara Brenner *pages 24–39*

Barbara Brenner has written over 40 children's books. She gets her ideas from a variety of places. Her love of science and nature has led her to write many books with animals in them. She gets other ideas from books she reads, children she knows, and the many different places she has lived. She spent several years in New York City, where *Mystery of the Plumed Serpent* is set.

Walter de la Mare *pages 22–23*

With the publication of *Peacock Pie* in 1994, a whole new generation of readers discovered Walter de la Mare's poems. The English author's first book of poetry was published in 1906. He went on to write hundreds of children's poems and short stories. De la Mare believed that poetry didn't have to be dry and dull, and that children didn't have to wait until they grew up to enjoy it. De la Mare died in 1956.

Sid Fleischman *pages 46–67*

This writer knows that it pays to have a few tricks up your sleeve when you're writing a mystery novel. Sid Fleischman was once a magician in a traveling vaudeville show. Many of Fleischman's novels—like the Newbery Award-winning *Whipping Boy*—contain mysterious twists and turns that keep the reader guessing. Fleischman likes to write books in series about the same characters. He's written five novels about the Bloodhound Gang.

Doris Rodriguez *pages 24–39*

This illustrator has vivid memories of her childhood, which led her to do a series of paintings about growing up in the Dominican Republic. For *Mystery of the Plumed Serpent*, Doris Rodriguez had to dig a little deeper to research her illustrations. She went to the Museum of Natural History in New York and made sketches of Aztec characters and designs.

Chris Van Allsburg *pages 10–19*

This Caldecott Award-winning author and illustrator is well known for creating books that are like puzzles for his readers to solve. At first, Chris Van Allsburg's mysterious drawings were only a hobby. His wife, a teacher, convinced him to turn them into children's books. Van Allsburg's readers must be glad she did. He gets hundreds of letters from young fans each year.

Books &

Author Study

More by Sid Fleischman

By the Great Horned Spoon
Jack and his aunt's butler, Praiseworthy, head for adventure in California during the Gold Rush era.

Jim Ugly
Twelve-year-old Jake Bannoch refuses to believe that his father is dead. He sets out with Jim Ugly, his father's dog, to find out the truth in this novel set in the Old West.

The Whipping Boy
A case of mistaken identity leads a prince and a servant boy to trade places in this funny, Newbery Award-winning novel.

Sid Fleischman

Fiction

Meg MacIntosh and the Mystery at the Medieval Castle
by Lucinda Landon
In this fast-paced mystery, picture clues help you— and Meg—solve the mystery.

Spider Kane and the Mystery at Jumbo Nightcrawlers
by Mary Pope Osborne
Insect investigator Spider Kane and his flying friends unravel the mystery when their friends disappear.

Who Really Killed Cock Robin? An Ecological Mystery
by Jean Craighead George
Saddleboro's most famous bird is dead and Tony sets out to investigate what sort of environmental imbalance could have led to its death.

Nonfiction

Pinkerton, America's First Private Eye
by Richard Pinkerton
This biography covers important events in Pinkerton's career and explains the methods that made the Pinkerton Detective Agency the best in the country.

Navaho Code Talkers
by Nathan Aaseng
Navaho intelligence agents, working for the United States military during World War II, used their own language to send secret messages. This Navaho code proved to be impossible for enemy nations to crack.

Tales Mummies Tell
by Patricia Lauber
This remarkable book reveals how scientists have studied mummies to learn a great deal about life in ancient times.

xMedia

Videos

Brother Future
Public Media
This WonderWorks production tells the story of T.J., who finds himself transported back in time from 1990s Detroit to South Carolina in the early 1800s. Now T.J. is a slave! During his adventure in the past, he helps organize a slave rebellion, and enlists the help of others to solve the mystery of why he traveled back in time, and how he can get back to the future.
(110 minutes)

The Hideaways
Warner Home Videos
Claudia and her younger brother become involved in a mystery at the Metropolitan Museum of Art. This adaptation of E. L. Konigsburg's wonderful book, *From The Mixed Up Files of Mrs. Basil E. Frankweiler,* is lots of fun.
(105 minutes)

Software

Ace Detective
Mind Play
(Apple, IBM, Macintosh)
You're the detective and your job is to analyze clues, organize information, and draw conclusions. Can you solve the mystery before time runs out?

The Secret Code of Cypher: Operation Wildlife
Tanager
(IBM, Macintosh)
Your mission is to decode a secret message. You'll discover a lot of information about animals as you follow a trail of clues through city streets and wildlife habitats.

Where in Time Is Carmen Sandiego?
Broderbund Software
(Macintosh, IBM)
Learn history and geography as you track Carmen, the quadruple agent for so many countries she has forgotten which one she is working for.

Magazines

DynaMath
Scholastic Inc.
It takes logic to solve a mystery. This magazine is full of entertaining activities and stories designed to help sharpen math and logic skills.

Kid City
Children's Television Workshop
Kid City has a little bit of everything involving reading and writing. Each issue focuses on a theme such as disguise, treasure, or mystery.

A Place to Write

American Jr. Academy of Science, Biology Dept., University of Richmond, Richmond, VA 23173

Write to The American Jr. Academy of Science to find out about state and local clubs for kids interested in scientific investigation.

Acknowledgments

Grateful acknowledgment is made to the following sources for permission to reprint from previously published material. The publisher has made diligent efforts to trace the ownership of all copyrighted material in this volume and believes that all necessary permissions have been secured. If any errors or omissions have inadvertently been made, proper corrections will gladly be made in future editions.

Cover: Untitled illustration #7 from "The West Wing" by Edward Gorey published in AMPHIGOREY: FIFTEEN BOOKS by Edward Gorey. Published by Perigee Books/G.P. Putnam's Sons. Copyright © 1963 by Edward Gorey. Reprinted by permission of Donadio & Ashworth, Inc.

Interior: Selections and cover from THE MYSTERIES OF HARRIS BURDICK by Chris Van Allsburg. Copyright © 1984 by Chris Van Allsburg. Reprinted by permission of Houghton Mifflin Company. All rights reserved.

Illustration for "Some One" and book cover from PEACOCK PIE. Text copyright © 1969 by The Literary Trustees of Walter de la Mare. Illustrations copyright © 1989 by Louise Brierley. Reprinted by permission of Henry Holt and Co., Inc.

Dramatization by Gary Drevitch of MYSTERY OF THE PLUMED SERPENT by Barbara Brenner. Original version text copyright © 1972 by Houghton Mifflin Company. Cover art copyright © 1981 by Judy Clifford. Reprinted by permission of Houghton Mifflin Company. All rights reserved.

Selection from WILL SHORTZ'S BEST BRAIN BUSTERS by Will Shortz. Copyright © 1991 by B & P Publishing Co. Reprinted by permission of Times Books, a division of Random House, Inc.

"The Case of the Secret Message" from THE CASE OF THE SECRET MESSAGE by Sid Fleischman. Copyright © 1981 by Children's Television Workshop. Reprinted by arrangement with Random House, Inc.

"Pointing a Finger" and cover from POLICE LAB: USING SCIENCE TO SOLVE CRIMES by Robert Sheely. Copyright © 1993 by Robert Sheely. Reprinted by permission of Silver Moon Press.

"The Case of the Buried Treasure" from TWO-MINUTE MYSTERIES by Donald J. Sobol. Copyright © 1967 by Donald J. Sobol. Published by Scholastic Book Services. Reprinted by permission of McIntosh and Otis, Inc.

Selection and cover from THE SECRETS OF VESUVIUS by Sara C. Bisel with Jane Bisel and Shelley Tanaka. Design and compilation copyright © 1990 The Madison Press Ltd. Text copyright © 1990 by Sara C. Bisel and family and The Madison Press Ltd. Reprinted by permission of The Madison Press Ltd.

Masthead from *The Boston Globe* and selections and chart adapted from *The Boston Globe*, March 19, 20 and May 13, 1990. Copyright © 1990 by *The Boston Globe*. Reprinted courtesy of *The Boston Globe*.

Cover from BURIED IN ICE: THE MYSTERY OF A LOST ARCTIC EXPEDITION by Owen Beattie and John Geiger. Illustration by W. H. Smyth; left photograph by Owen Beattie, the National Maritime Museum; middle illustration by the Bridgeman/Art Resource; right photograph by Owen Beattie. Photographs copyright © 1992 by Owen Beattie. Cover design and compilation copyright © 1992 by The Madison Press Ltd. Published by Madison Press Books.

Cover from FROM THE MIXED-UP FILES OF MRS. BASIL E. FRANKWEILER by E. L. Konigsburg. Illustration copyright © 1977 by Dell Publishing, a division of Bantam Doubleday Dell Publishing Group, Inc.

Cover from SUSANNAH AND THE PURPLE MONGOOSE MYSTERY by Patricia Elmore, illustrated by Bob Marstall. Illustration copyright © 1992 by Bob Marstall. Reprinted by permission of Dutton Children's Books, a division of Penguin Books USA Inc.

Cover from WINDCATCHER by Avi. Illustration copyright © 1992 by Avon Books. Published by Avon Books, a division of The Hearst Corporation.

Photography and Illustration Credits

Photos: © John Lei for Scholastic Inc., All Tool Box items unless otherwise noted. p. 2-3: © Bill Barley for Scholastic Inc., except for p. 3 bc: © Laurence Dutton/Tony Stone Images, Inc.; tc: © Ana Esperanza Nance for Scholastic Inc. p. 4 © Ana Esperanza Nance for Scholastic Inc.; tc: © Laurence Dutton/Tony Stone Images, Inc. p. 5 c: © Ana Esperanza Nance for Scholastic Inc.; tc: © Laurence Dutton/Tony Stone Images, Inc. p. 6 c: © Francis Clark Westfield for Scholastic Inc.; tc: © Laurence Dutton/Tony Stone Images, Inc. p. 20 Barbara Steil: Courtesy of Barbara Steil; James Campbell: © F. Carter Smith for Scholastic Inc.; Myriam Rodriguez: © David Phillips; Tim Leatherman: Courtesy of Tim Leatherman; Lensey Namioka: Courtesy of Lensey Namioka. p. 42 br: © Stanley Bach for Scholastic Inc. p. 43 br: © Bill Barley for Scholastic Inc. p. 68 bl: Halley Ganges for Scholastic Inc. p. 70 tl: © Mark Burnett/Photo Researchers, Inc. p. 72 bc: © Russ Kinne/Comstock, Inc. p. 73 bc: © Ed Kashi/Phototake NYC. pp. 74-75: © John Lei for Scholastic Inc. p. 78 c: © Laurence Dutton/Tony Stone Images, Inc.; all others: © Bill Barley for Scholastic Inc. pp. 79-81: © Bill Barley for Scholastic Inc. pp. 82-83: © John Lei for Scholastic Inc. p. 84 © Stanley Bach for Scholastic Inc. p. 85 br: © Bill Barley for Scholastic Inc. p. 88 bl: © Cheryl Nuss/National Geographic Society; br: © Jonathan Blair/National Geographic Society. p. 91 bc: © O. Louis Mazzatenta/National Geographic Society. p. 92 br: © Cheryl Nuss/National Geographic Society. p. 93 c: © Jonathan Blair/National Geographic Society. p. 95 tl: © O. Louis Mazzatenta/National Geographic Society. p. 97 tc: © O. Louis Mazzatenta/National Geographic Society. p. 99 bl: © Cheryl Nuss/National Geographic Society. pp. 100-101: © O. Louis Mazzatenta/National Geographic Society. p. 102 c: © AP/Wide World Photos. p. 103 cr: © *The Concert*, Jan Vermeer/Isabella Stewart Gardner Museum, Boston. p. 105 bl: © Springer/The Bettmann Film Archive. p. 107 tc: © Arrow Map, Inc./Bie Bostrom for Scholastic Inc.; br: © Mark Hunt/Isabella Stewart Gardner Museum, Boston/Light Sources. p. 110 br: © Isabella Stewart Gardner Museum, Boston. p. 112 tc: courtesy of House of Mystery at the Oregon Vortex in Gold Hill, OR; c: © Lynn Hughes/Liaison International; bc: Luis Castañeda/The Image Bank. p. 113 c: © UPI/The Bettmann Archive; bc: © Topkapi Palace Museum. pp. 114-115 bc: © Cosimo Condina/Tony Stone Images Inc.; tr: © Charles Henneghien/Bruce Coleman, Inc. p. 115 c: © Bruce Stoddard/FPG International Corp.; br: © Kathleen Campbell/Tony Stone Images, Inc. pp. 116-117 tc: © Bob Torrez/Tony Stone Images, Inc. p. 116 bl: © Stanley Bach for Scholastic Inc. bc: © John Lei for Scholastic Inc. p. 117 bl: © Stanley Bach for Scholastic Inc. p. 118 cr: © David Hiser/Tony Stone Images, Inc. p. 119 br: © Bill Barley for Scholastic Inc. p. 120 cr: © George Gerster/Comstock, Inc. p. 121 c: © Robert Noonan/Photo Researchers, Inc.; bl: © D. Bartruff/FPG International Corp. p. 122 cl: © Gary Buss/FPG International Corp. p. 123 tr: © James H. Carmichael, Jr./Photo Researchers, Inc.; bc: © Frank Cruz for Scholastic Inc. p. 124 tl: © Sara Bisel; cl: © Henry Holt & Company; bl: © Mark Gerson. p. 125 tr: © Becky Mojica; cr: © Donna F. Aceto for Scholastic Inc.; br: © Houghton Mifflin/Chris Van Allsburg. p. 126 bl: © Becky Mojica. p. 127 br: © Stanley Bach for Scholastic Inc.

Illustrations: pp. 8-9: John O'Brien; pp. 24-39: Doris Rodriguez; p. 41: Bernard Adnet; pp. 44-45: John O'Brien; pp. 46-67: Ken Barr; pp. 76-77: Mike Quon; pp. 86-87: John O'Brien; pp. 102-111: Pronto Design; pp. 112-113: Steven Stankiewicz.